Anna

A Novel by
SUSAN
EVANS
McCLOUD

BOOKCRAFT
Salt Lake City, Utah

Library of Congress Catalog Card Number: 86-64021
ISBN 0-88494-855-2

Second Paperback Printing, 1992

Printed in the United States of America

This one belongs to my sister, Dianne,
and the years of dreaming we shared together

Chapter One

It was a raw night for April. I remember it clearly. The house seemed to rock with the force of the wind, and make shudders of protest. We sat huddled around the fire listening to stories as a gale blew in off the sea, wet and noisy. I like the sounds of the sea, even when it's angry. But my grandfather's story disturbed me nevertheless.

His voice was deep and resonant, the voice of a singer, and its rise and fall had a cadence that might have lulled me if the tragedy of his words had not been so stark.

"It was a winter with teeth to its bite like you've never seen, Anna." He nodded in my direction and I nodded back. My brother Petur stirred in the shadows beside me. "We had used up all the dried fish," my grandfather continued. "The sour butter and *hafkal* were gone, too." He shook his head, and the old lines of sorrow cut deep in his forehead. "A day came without storm. The skies seemed milder. Other years we might have waited, but not this year. My brother, Petur, was the best sailor among us. You are like him," he said to the shadows beside me. "Resilient and hopeful and sure of yourself." I could almost feel Petur smile. Such praises pleased him. "He took his sons, Lofter and Thordur, with him, and my own son, Samuel." My grandfather sighed. I knew what was coming next, and I didn't like it. But the story must wind itself out to the end, with no one thinking to stop or amend its telling.

"I walked to the edge of the sea with them. The cloud shadows spotted the water, green pools on the surface of a sea that was gray and unsettled. We pushed the boat in at the edge of the cove. The waves, where the rocks stopped them, pounded nine feet, ten feet high in their anger, and the spray from the waves was cold on my skin."

My grandfather made a clucking noise back in his throat and shook his head. His long white hair seemed sprinkled with shimmering flecks that danced and trembled.

"I would have gone in place of the boys," he continued. His voice had lowered, and a hollow tone had crept in. "But your father there seemed anxious to enter the world, so I stayed with his mother. They meant to cast their lines near the shallows—I don't know what happened. One moment young Samuel was waving his hand, his face glowing with pleasure . . . the next moment the boat seemed to rise on the back of a monster—"

My baby sister cried out in her sleep and I felt my skin prickle.

"I watched helplessly while the boat lunged out to the sea, a toy for the waves to play with. The next wave" —his words were like stones—"they went under, effortlessly, with no noise, no protest. Though I watched till my eyes stung and blurred, I saw no trace of them. They never came up again."

I gazed into the fire where the peat curled into small flames. I could end the story without listening to his words.

"I went home to my Hela," he continued, "and told her our son was lost. But before the night fell, the gods blessed our home with a new son. And so the pain did not swallow your grandmother's heart, my Anna. And thus the gods give, and the gods take away. And man learns to live with the gods and their pleasure."

His voice ended. The whale-oil lamp sputtered. I thought the shadows looked deep and cold. I leaned against Petur, and closed my eyes because they were stinging a little. I didn't hear the sound at the door, but my father heard it. He rose noiselessly from his place and crossed the room with the stealthy skill of our cat that now slept in the corner. Our eyes, all our eyes, followed after my father. And everyone's breath seemed to hover and hold.

He called through the latch, "Who is there?" and the muffled answer was lost in the cold rush of wind that blew into the kitchen. I saw the two young men bend over to pass through the door, and my father hasten to shut it behind them. One of them grinned and pushed his hat back off his forehead. He was the one I liked best. I sat up to listen.

"No spies out in a storm like this one!" His friendly grin widened.

"None out but the foolhardy, yes—and those up to mischief."
My grandfather said the words slowly. There was no music in
them.

"I plead guilty to the first designation, sir. That I must do."
Elder Thorderson laughed and shrugged his big shoulders. "We
had to come tonight, Einar." He turned now to my father and
lowered his voice a little. "The meeting's tomorrow, just after
chores in the morning. The usual place. We should receive all the
final details we need for leaving. Very important."

"I'll be there," my father said.

"And Margret. I think Margret should come as well. There
will be things for the women's ears."

"I'll go in her place." I had said the words without thinking to
say them.

Elder Thorderson turned his warm eyes upon me and my
father looked me thoughtfully up and down.

"Perhaps, daughter, if the baby is still unwell, and your mother
wishes."

He turned his back then and drew the two young men closer.
What he told them was not for our ears, but I could feel it, as I had
felt the cold spray from the sea that had drenched our grandfather,
as I had felt the wild ache in his heart as he turned his steps home. I
knew my father would be telling the missionaries of our troubles
with the Lutheran minister, how last week he had spoken from the
very pulpit to denounce the Mormons, with bitter words that
were harsh and untrue. And how, after the service was out, not
one of our neighbors spoke a word of greeting to us, and on the
road the little pony that pulled our cart caught a stone in his hoof,
and the people passed in a wide path around us, and not one of
them offered us help.

It was hard for my father, perhaps harder than for the rest of
us, even my mother. We waited a few moments longer, trying not
to listen, then my mother rose from her chair and went to the cupboard and pulled out two wooden bowls and a small cask of *skyr*.
She ladled the sweet curds into the bowls with a generous hand
and presented them, along with spoons, to the two standing men,
who took them with grateful smiles and then ate as they listened.

My mother turned, and at a motion of her head the younger
children, Gesli, Sina, and Samuel, began to move, finding their

4

places on the narrow shelf beds they slept on. I tried to avoid her eyes, but she wouldn't have it.

"Anna," she instructed, "take the small lamp with you and tuck the children into bed."

"Shall I hear their prayers?"

She hesitated a moment, and I wondered if she prayed to the Heavenly Father the Elders taught of, and if she was comfortable with such praying.

"Yes, dear, if you would."

She dismissed me with the words, and my desires had no place in the hard scheme of schedule. I noticed that Petur had moved out from his corner and close to the men. I might have complained of such unfair treatment—Petur was only one year my senior— but *he* was listening, the young Elder with the dancing blue eyes. He mustn't see me as a whiner and a baby.

I took up the stone dish a little abruptly. The cotton wick danced in the whale oil. I tried to walk with the same fluid grace as the oil, for perhaps he was watching, though why he should be watching I didn't know. But if by chance his eyes fell upon me, I mustn't look the awkward girl I was feeling inside.

I turned my gaze to the beds where the children waited and tried to concentrate on the prayers they were saying, and their warm little lips on my cheek. But before they had freed me I felt a cold draft of air at my back and turned in time to catch only a glimpse of him—cheekbone, profile, thatch of thick yellow hair, then his sturdy back, then the black door that shut him out. I turned back to the children. It was silent now. It was much too silent. The wind bleated outside the house like a frightened lamb. And the fear, like the chill, played along my skin.

My grandfather did not go to the Mormon meeting the following morning. He had not been baptized as the rest of us had. Nor was he immigrating to Zion. His life in Iceland, though long and hard, was now near its end. He belonged here. Here, in the soil of the island, lay buried his mother, his father, his wife, and three of his children. Here he had lived out his hopes and dreams. I think he resented the fact that his youngest son was deserting those dreams, adopting dreams that were foreign to him. But he never protested, he never stood in the way or made accusations.

Whatever he endured, he endured without losing his dignity. He was that kind of a man, my grandfather. I loved him dearly.

The Vestmaneyjar or Westmann Islands lie off the southern coast of Iceland about twelve miles. They begin far down in the sea and they have a history as wild as the water that spawned them, and a people as secretive and proud as the ocean itself. A world apart. That was what we were. Even those on the mainland recognized and respected our ways. We fished and kept long-wooled sheep and we farmed a little, held here not by the ease of the place, but by its beauty: fierce and stark as the black jagged cliffs, and gentle as the gentians and harebells that bloom in the spring, when the wind blows the clouds away in a glory of rainbows and the air is as fresh as the first springs on earth must have been.

I love the island. I had never intended to set foot off Heimaey as long as I lived. I took the path that morning with mixed feelings. For all my seventeen years I was in most ways a child, and the sensations uppermost in my mind revolved around the thrill of seeing the handsome missionary again and the honor of having a place among the women.

I met no one on the path. It was the custom of the Saints to approach the grassy, level valley one at a time by the numerous paths and roads that led there. That way we avoided our persecutors and kept our affairs to ourselves. This morning the mountain walls enclosing the valley gleamed like black silk and the sky above our heads shone as blue as the ocean. As I drew closer the sun caught the red in the cliffside and the bright yellow splashes of buttercups and the purple of vetch. Just then a flock of white gannets stretched out above me, and I watched the magnificent slash of bright wings slowly feather the air with a grace that awed me. My breath caught in my throat. What was I doing? What madness this talk about ships and journeys, wagons with white sails pulled behind oxen, prairie grass and buffalo! What was I doing? What was my father having us do?

At the meeting I took down careful instructions to carry back to Mother. We'd be traveling lightly. They stressed the importance of that: we were cutting all cords. Would we leave more of ourselves behind than we took along with us? I wondered—but I did not put words to the fear.

The meeting was brief and the missionaries were busy with questions on top of each other, too many to answer. I nodded to my father and walked from the valley up a steep, narrow path that did not lead home. From here I looked down on the gentle bays and the dark sands that edged them, and the ache in my heart was too sharp to bear. Zion was only a name. I could never imagine what it would be like to live on a desert, in some other land. Couldn't we be Latter-day Saints in Iceland? Did it matter so much what they thought of us here? Perhaps I should ask my father that question. Didn't the Island of West Men need God on it, too? Couldn't we serve him here as well as in Zion?

Zion. The word was a burden to utter. I would speak to my father this very day. Perhaps he felt the same way I did. Perhaps he would think again about going to Zion.

Chapter Two

It was late evening before I could catch my father. The sea was red with the sun, the cliffs were golden, as though lit with a torch from within. All the land was in silence. My father stood alone in the silence and watched the night push the sun off the edge of the world. I went to my father and stood beside him for a moment before I could speak.

"I don't think the deserts in the land called Zion have sunsets like this one."

He did not answer me, so I went a step further. "I think the islands need God in them, too, Father. Why can't we be Latter-day Saints here?"

His movement in turning to me had a painfulness in it. I had never seen tears in his eyes before.

"The islands were born with God in them, daughter." His voice was so low that I strained to hear it. "God is the breath of the islands, and though man can drown it, he cannot destroy its sweet rhythm. No, daughter. The islands have what they need. But Zion —Zion has what *we* need."

I shook tears from my eyes. "*I* need the island, Father! The island and the sea—I can't live without them."

"We shall try, you and I," he said. And I knew at that moment that indeed his heart was breaking along with mine. And I knew there was no hope, and I ran up the hillside and lay in the moss and cried till my mother found me.

"Come to bed." Her touch was cool, but her voice was firm.

"I don't want to go to Zion," I said.

"People do what they don't want to do; that is living, Anna. We are Icelanders, bred to the hard way. Always the harsh, the untamed for us. Always the struggle. It is the way . . ." She pulled at my hand. "Come, Anna. And a smile for your father, you hear?"

I nodded, and followed her down the hill and through our gate and into the house I loved. And my heart cried inside me. But my eyes were dry and I smiled at my father. Alone in my bed, I forbade the tears to come. I would be like my mother and close my heart to the pain. But I didn't know how, and the tears had their way with me and the crying eased the suffering a bit, and I slept.

I had a friend in Iceland named Halldor, a girl my age. We met nearly every day, and my last weeks on the island were made more difficult by those meetings. I dared not tell her the things that were coming to pass; I dared not confide the tender feelings I was suffering. We worked together, at sewing and mending and cleaning. We played together, running the length of the shore with the spray in our faces and the sound of the sea in our ears, in our heads. Where the far cliffs seemed to blossom with stout, white-breasted puffin we watched the toylike birds with their bright-colored bills and made girlish plans for a future that never would be. The cloud I walked in, the cloud I smothered in was my own. It did not obscure the happy sunshine of Halldor's days. So I basked in sunlight borrowed from her and held my peace. And the dreaded day of departure drew nearer.

Petur was in a daze of enthusiasm. He was almost an embarrassment at times. So many new adventures—he used to count them—more than he had fingers, all coming to him. One could not help but smile to watch him. At times I envied him his pleasure. After all, he was a boy, with that itching for freedom. The things I would leave behind that tugged at my heart—these meant nothing to him. Nor did the bulk of the preparations fall to the men. Food and clothing and household chores—that was woman's realm.

It seemed every day I discovered another treasure for Mother and me to set carefully in the cupboard and leave for Grandfather. Essentials. Only essentials. Only practical things would go. I slipped in all the books I could, though my mother warned me that we must learn to speak the English now. I tucked in the doll my grandmother had made and the worn gold earrings that had come from Norway with my mother's people, the original Stefanssons, long ago.

I knew my mother had tucked in some things of her own when she thought no one was watching. But oh, so much, so much we loved must be left behind. My grandfather, watching our movements, said to my mother, "I will keep these for you, Margret, never fear." He bent over and kissed her cheek. "God will protect you. Perhaps one day . . ."

It was a way of cheating the pain, just a little.

Did anyone know what we planned, or guess at it? I suppose there were those who knew, more and more as the time drew nearer. Would there be trouble? Would the people grow angry and nasty? The Lutheran minister stopped by to see us one Saturday evening. He was brusque and his eyebrows frowned and his eyes were stormy.

"You still listen to those Mormons, Einar—you expose your family—you poison your children's minds!" His voice was shaking.

"You shame your own kind," he accused, "and you bring dishonor on the sacred memory of your ancestors." He spoke with venom. "Come to your senses, Einar, forsake this madness! It will bring ruin upon your heads. Arni—" He turned to my grandfather with an eloquent gesture of helplessness. "Old friend, can you not talk some sense into this young man?"

My grandfather sighed. "He is not a young man, Sveinn, and as far as sense goes, I believe he has as much as he'll ever have."

I thought I saw light in my father's eyes, but the gray-haired pastor—the same man who had dragged the missionaries to answer before the magistrates of the law, who had told lies about them and forbidden them shelter—went away dark and muttering to himself. And a coldness crept into the room with his leaving that even my mother's hot *rengi* could not dispel.

"Will there be whale meat in Zion?" little Gesli asked.

"No," I told him. "There will not be whales in Zion, or seals or cod, or kittiwakes or puffins along the cliffs or—"

"Anna." My mother's voice was stern and quiet. "Eat your food."

The missionaries had said we would like it in Utah. But I was not convinced. I liked it here. And I'm not the kind who cares much for change or surprises.

"There will be buffalo," Petur grinned, "ten times as big as the sheep here and as shaggy as your wooliest lamb. And better to eat, they say, than whales. And there will be mountains—taller than these—"

He had Gesli smiling before I could swallow the bite I was chewing. *Let him be happy,* I thought to myself. *Let him be happy as long as he can.*

Then there was the baby. Dena was my special domain, but I didn't mind. She was as chubby and round as a fledgling puffin and as squirmy as a newborn puppy. I couldn't see how we'd ever keep track of her on so long a journey. Yet tending her wasn't a chore; she was that precious, the apple of everyone's eye, and she knew it. And though she took advantage, to see her smile, to feel her arms around your neck made the care and the effort worth it, ten times over.

So we became ready, day by day, task by task. I was forsaking everything I could think of in life to love: my island, my home, my friends, my grandfather. Even the cat I had raised from a kitten, and the handsome young Elder Thorderson, who would not be coming to Zion with us. How could I hope to carry it all inside me, and not perish from the keeping?

The day arrived. I awoke that morning with the sound of the sea in my ears. I walked down to the cove, my eyes stinging with the gazing at every inch, so I might burn the sights into my mind forever. *The sea.* Waking and sleeping the sea was with us—the demon, the mysterious stranger, the life-giving friend, the enemy, the enchantress.

When the time came for leaving we left by the sea. Twenty-six of us Saints, a small number huddled awkwardly together with boxes and bags. Some of the converts had mothers and fathers and brothers and sisters who had disowned them, who already looked upon them as lost, as dead. I especially remember one young woman who stood alone with her thin arms around two little girls, crying, "Mother, Mother, I love you, Mother."

My grandfather came to the edge of the sea—to the edge of the world—with us. We would never see him alive again. We all knew it. He kissed my mother and all of us children. He embraced his son and rocked him back and forth in his arms for a moment. He watched our ship pull away from the sand and push into the water. He stood there, just as he had on that day long before, watching the sea take his son from him. But today there was no one waiting to welcome him home. Today, when he turned, red-eyed and exhausted, there would be no loving arms to hold him, no voice, no face. Only memory and shadow.

I stood and watched—I watched and watched till the blur on the shoreline faded and then disappeared. There was nothing. Nothing but water and sky. I closed my eyes. I would carry my grandfather's face with me to Zion. I would carry the sound of the sea inside me as long as I lived.

Chapter Three

We left Iceland forever on the day of June 6, 1856. Fifteen days later we arrived safely in Liverpool, England. If that had been all of the journey, I would have been happy. Petur was all over the ship, poking his nose in, getting in everyone's way, asking questions. I wasn't like that, I'm sorry to admit. I like hearth and home. And besides, I had the care of the baby. Little Dena didn't get sick from the motion beneath her, but she didn't sit still for one minute, it seemed. I did walk long stretches of deck with her, looking off to where gray sky met gray sea, wondering what my grandfather was doing back home on the island. They would be fishing the cod and the herring now, and perhaps the shoals of halibut. He would be busy, with work for his hands to do. I was grateful for that.

I don't remember much about England. We were there only for a few days and most of that time was not spent in sightseeing. I do remember walking the streets once when flags hung down from the houses and coaches drove by, and the people came to their windows and doorways and shouted, and those on the streets began singing a tune. The words were English words—I've since learned them, *God save our gracious Queen*—but the tune was Icelandic. It formed an instant lump in my throat. *Eldgamla Isafold*, our national hymn—I had often sung it, liking the feel of the slow, solid music inside my head. Now to know that these pale, pinched-face Englanders sang it!

We left without much fanfare or ceremony on a day that was neither cloudy nor fair, just a plain day, with nothing special to mark it. We slipped away into the sea, unremarked, unremembered. The Church had placed agents in Liverpool and they knew their business. They had done this how many dozens of times before? They chartered a vessel exclusively for our people, and appointed a president over the ship's company, with lesser officers in line under the leader. It worked well. There was order among us and, if we were strangers, at least we were brothers and sisters with some things in common.

The journey was probably fair as such journeys go. The two things I found hardest to suffer were the poor food and the poor sanitary conditions. Breakfast is the most important meal in Iceland. *Dagmal*, we call it, the day meal. How can one start the day without food in his belly? Not a slab of stale bread and a tasteless mush, but solid food that will stay in your stomach. I missed fresh fish and fresh milk. And also, I missed the hot springs where we washed our clothes. They would come out of the wash pure and white, fresh smelling, so you would hold them against your nose and put your face down into them. I disliked the smell of unwashed bodies, unwashed clothing, unwashed babies. I suppose I was spoiled a little, yet still it was hard.

We should have been learning the English on shipboard. My mother said so a hundred times. But it was difficult to make friends with the others. Each kept pretty much to his own group. And most of the ones on our ship already spoke English. Mother said we ought to try harder—smile more often, ask questions. But how to do that, when there were no words inside your head to ask questions with? My father and some of the men did a little better, working beside the others from time to time. Petur was most at ease among them. He made friends, and he picked things up quickly. He'd bring back words—two or three, maybe six or seven a day. Some of the words were shipboard words: *deck, rope, cabin, mainsail*—terms for the sea.

Once he came up to me and touched little Dena. *Baby,* he said —*bay-bee.* That one was easy. *Brother, sister, mother,* and *father* came harder. *Nose, eyes, hair*—he helped the time pass. *Foot, shoe, toe:* we wrote out the words, and when the president learned of our interest he helped us further, and his pretty, quiet wife sat with us for hours until the English words we knew rose to quite a number. I used to count them, but very soon I lost track. Icelanders are language-proud. Our most common people are educated to read and write. Most of the great writings of the world our men translated so we might read them in pure Icelandic. Thus, this word game was more than learning so we could adjust to a new way of life. It was a matter of keeping our self-respect and our ancient pride.

July eleventh we took ship. Six weeks later, on August the twenty-fourth, we pulled into port. Philadelphia: one of America's oldest cities. But then, the land was an infant compared to Iceland.

There was confusion there. I remember confusion, crowds of people talking and jostling each other. The relief of getting off ship was dulled with confusion, and the English words I knew didn't seem to help—one or two to recognize out of dozens and dozens.

Philadelphia marked the end and the beginning. Nothing past that till we reached the Valley would matter again.

We stood in the crowded station waiting for Father, who was seeing, with some of the men, to our travel arrangements. We must connect in this city with a train to take our group on to St. Louis. I admit to a certain degree of excitement at that—to ride upon one of those fast, black, noisy monsters!

Perhaps that was on my mind. Perhaps I was tired—I know I was tired. I had given the baby to Mother to hold. She had wanted Mother, held her arms out, and who could resist her? But then little Sina, not much more than a baby herself, fell and scraped her knee. She had been running when Mother told her not to. I had bent down to scold and comfort a little. Just then they told us to move our luggage to a new section. Petur began to pick up all he could. Mother tried to help him, but with the baby in her arms there was not much she could do.

All at once. Ten thousand times I've lived through it. If I had straightened up a few seconds sooner. If Mother had waited a heartbeat more and called out to me. If Sina hadn't been crying so loudly. If Petur had not turned his back, with his arms full of bags. . . .

A stranger, a man, stood beside my mother. "I'll hold that baby for you, ma'am." His face looked kind. Only Mother saw his face, not I nor Petur. Only she saw the warmth in the man's eyes. She handed Dena to him with some reluctance.

"A moment," she said, pointing to our bags. He nodded. "No need to hurry. She's sure a darlin'."

"Thank you," Mother murmured. She turned from the man. She took Gesli by one hand and a bag in the other, instructing me to do the same. I dragged Sina with me. Samuel trailed behind, his arms filled, too. It was moments, only moments! We found Petur and moved the bags to where he stood. He went with Mother to get the last heavy crate and the squirming baby. The crate sat squat on the spot where we had left it. The man with the kindly face was nowhere to be found.

At first there was little alarm. Mother looked for the stranger. He was tall. She could find her own baby held high in his arms. She looked, but there were so many people! Petur, searching with her, called out the name: "Dena . . . Dena . . . precious . . . come to your Petur!" I heard the name and went cold inside. Something within me knew. I cried out to my mother. She turned. I shall never forget her eyes.

I think I must have screamed. I couldn't help it. Then the confusion grew thick and close. People asking us questions, trying to help—one blue-coated official. I struggled to tell him. Suddenly someone caught the drift. Perhaps the woman, the young woman with pale, wide eyes.

"Her baby's been stolen! Some man was holding her baby, and now he's gone!"

People turned, strangers joined my mother in searching. No one knew exactly what they were looking for. A tall man holding a baby—any baby. A chubby-cheeked, dark-haired baby from Iceland who cried in a different language from theirs. Any man— any tall, kindly man out of dozens!

I didn't notice when Father came. I scarcely noticed when we moved outside the building, away from the crowds. I went woodenly with the others. Another station. The black monster, long and sleek, grumbled under its breath, breathing steam out of dozens of spewing nostrils.

We missed the first train. We stayed all night in the little depot. We must have slept, we must have eaten something. I don't remember. I wanted to go with my father, but Mother went. Every man in our company went. There was no use in going. The man had meant to take the child. But how cruel is hope! Perhaps he had changed his mind! Perhaps he had left her in some out-of-the-way corner!

The officials were more than kind. Everyone helped us. The blue-coated officers showed our men how to put an advertisement in the newspaper, and all pooled from their little store a sum for reward. Sina cried out in the night. When I heard her, more than halfway asleep myself, I thought it was Dena. I called to her, searching the blankets beside me. *She's here—the baby's back,* my mind cried. *I must find Mother and tell her!*

And then I awoke. And I could not sleep again, for I knew my Dena was crying somewhere, in some stranger's house, calling for Anna, calling for Mother. And the strangers could not even understand what she cried!

I could not bear to think of her fear, her aloneness. My mind ached trying to fit itself around the thought that a person could steal someone else's baby—a real, warm, flesh-and-blood, cherished child!

The following morning our company left. We stayed two days longer. Nothing. No response to the newspaper advertisement. No lost children. No abandoned babies in corners. I thought: *If Grandfather knew, this would break his heart. Thank heaven he isn't here to go through this again!* Yet how my own torn, aching heart yearned for his comfort!

Our family took the train that would carry us to the city called St. Louis. No one mentioned any more little Dena's name. My father persuaded Mother to eat something. The younger children watched the new countryside with interest. I stared straight ahead and saw nothing. I felt nothing but a dull, dragging ache inside. My mother never cried, but her eyes were a nightmare of pain, and my father spent long hours staring out of the window, tears wet upon his cheeks.

We reached St. Louis. We transferred from there to a steamer and ended up at a place called Burlington, Iowa. Now the journey, the real journey to Zion, was all that was left us.

We had spent six weeks in our ship on the ocean. We spent that many months and more on the Iowa plains. We met the rest of our company there and that was some comfort. The men had plenty to fill their time. There was work they could do to earn money to buy an outfit: food, ammunition, a wagon, oxen to pull it—so many things. The women were busy, of course, with their baking and sewing, putting up what provisions they could for the long time ahead. And, of course, there was always the care of the children. Many of the women had babies. Of course. We did, too —but we could not talk of our baby. She was not dead and decently buried somewhere behind. We could not lament with the ones who had lost children that way. The pain was too fresh— the pain was a freak, it was not a healer. This kind of pain had no end. We knew that. It would never free us, as the pain of a grave that would gradually dim and find a soft, hallowed spot in the heart.

There were so many little things that were different about us. First and foremost beyond our speech was the way we dressed. All the clothing our men brought with them was made of wool.

The pantaloons and coats they wore were fashioned from sheep-skin, and they wore in bad weather a leather hood. We women wore broad scarves around our necks and shoulders, tied in bows in the front, and little caps on our heads. And the shoes we wore were of sheep or sealskin, one piece drawn over the foot with no heel. They resembled the Indian moccasins more than the white men's shoes. There were many who were anxious to laugh and point fingers at us. There is that breed of person wherever you go. But the ones who did not mock were in some ways crueler. They *avoided* us—kindly, politely. But all the same, we were often left very much to ourselves to be different, and lonely.

It would never have been as bad, not one portion, if it had not been for the loss of Dena. As it was, we were using most of our strength simply to struggle up from that anguish and keep on going. We had not the excitement nor the enthusiasm to ram our way into a world that was alien and indifferent to us.

Petur was, of course, the exception to that. The exuberance of an eighteen-year-old boy is hard to contain. He wanted to see everything, do everything, be all places at once. He worked some-times with Father and the other men, and if he was snubbed there, he could shake it off his shoulders.

"What do you expect?" he would ask. "We are different. It isn't their fault any more than it's ours. After a while they forget to make jokes and stare. It's not half bad, and it's something to do to put coins in our pockets.

"Besides," he'd add, wrinkling his nose at me, "this isn't Zion, Anna. This is just Iowa—so don't expect too much."

It helped. He drew us all out of the morbid, where it was so easy for us to stagnate and sink.

Cold. That Iowa winter was colder than anything I had felt back home. The Southwesterlies, warm Atlantic currents, wash our coast and lend us a breath of tropical air. We have thunder-storms and gales, but not bitter arctic temperatures, not in the south. Often the island is green year-round, and in early summer it is light on our island all day. The sun doesn't set till nearly midnight and rises at two, and even those hours are merely a twi-light that dims the earth, and darkness becomes a thing put aside and forgotten.

I don't remember seeing the sun that Iowa winter. It left in November and didn't come back. I don't remember seeing much, if the truth be known. It was bitter and barren: no sea, no mountains, nothing to break the stretch of horizon that affronted the eye. I remember only one thing of real beauty: the trees. Flowers can cling in the rocky crevices of our cliffsides, but a tree cannot hope to survive that way. I fell in love with the broad, massive trees of the flat lands. I thought there was poetry in their bare branches that raked the skies, black as spider-leg lace on the white pillow surface. At times I could hear the wind in the trees like music, and it eased my hunger for sounds of the sea. Mostly we all were homesick and unhappy. Zion was still something far-off and unreal. And home was becoming that way, too.

We did progress far in Iowa toward learning the English. Mother learned it fastest of all, I think as a weapon—against her pain, and against her feeling of separateness here. She was ever and always the realist among us. Once she found that the pain of Dena had left her alive, she looked about for ways to survive the shambles and make the best of her little store. That was always her way.

Spring came. Wet and muddy and graceless, but still, it came. Father worked with the other men making yokes for the oxen, boxes to store household goods, spokes for wagons. Father was good with tools: his mind and his hands were at ease then. I can scarcely thread a needle myself or pour candle wax neatly. Our men did all they could to cut expenses. April came with the sweetness of buds and the smell of black earth. The Iowa soil was a pleasure to run through your fingers. Mother planted a garden there, though she knew she would leave it. "A little gladness for someone to reap," she said. I think the planting itself for her was a balm and a gladness.

May came. No more rain, but the promise of hot days. We left Burlington on the fourteenth, and just one month later pulled into Council Bluffs. We were seasoned travelers. All the aches and pains were gone, all the boils and blisters, the first painful sunburn relayered with tan. We were ready for the last long leg of the journey: Council Bluffs to Salt Lake City—that mystical place where we would really see Brigham Young, a modern-day prophet, fresh water that ran through the city streets, a salty lake, and the site of a temple. Salt Lake City! Zion! Tomorrow! We could finally feel the taste of it on our tongues.

Chapter Four

Soon enough there was to be only one taste on our tongues: the taste of *dust!* The dust of the wagons ahead and the wagons behind, the dust of the prairie storms, of the passing travelers — the dust of the buffalo herds and our own herds of cattle, the dust of the dry riverbed — dust in hair and eyes, encrusted in hems of dresses, staining our petticoats, itching inside our stockings and shoes. Everything smacked of dust — it became the flavor of all we tasted, the texture of all we touched!

But in time even that was adjusted to and forgotten. We grew healthy and strong with the sun and exercise. Even our spirits, so long in travail, began to break free.

Our journey in crossing the plains was a saga in itself. We Icelanders — how we love a good story! We preserved our own history that way for hundreds of years. And honor was measured by the honesty of the speaker who wove his adventures strictly from accurate detail and fact. We wanted not tall tales to beguile our children, but spirit speaking to spirit across the years, so that flesh and blood would tingle and warm with the telling, and feel the courage and poetry of the past course like blood through their veins.

My family were vaguely aware of our place in the saga, the significance of transplanting a people from one wilderness to another: trading sea and rock, gales and ice storms for sand and sage, wind storms and sun. We had come here as Latter-day Saints, but we were Icelanders. Father had felt that we could not be Latter-day Saints in Iceland. But could we be Icelanders in Zion? The question was there. And I know my father considered the question, for he made sure we kept up on our reading and recited our lessons and told the stories so we would not forget.

Our company boasted sixty-eight wagons with 390 people in all. Floyd's Company we were called; William Floyd was our captain, and under him captains of hundred, captains of fifty, and captains of ten. My father was appointed a captain of fifty, over half of these Icelanders like ourselves. Thus he was their pastor, their shepherd, and he took the role very seriously. He also did what he could to unite his people with the Norwegian converts under his charge. One would think the task easy. We Icelanders were vassals under the Norwegian king, for most of Iceland was settled by sturdy Norwegians. Our roots were the same, our systems, our traditions, our ancient gods. In fact, it was the flower of Norway, the earls and nobles, who settled our land. But they brought with them a spirit of independence—a fierce longing for freedom ran through their veins. In the summer of the year 930 on the Plains of Assembly, at the place called Thingvellier, they established the *Althing*. While the feudal tribes of Europe warred against one another, hacking through civilizations and races to determine supremacy, with deliberate intent and without bloodshed our people established a solid democracy.

For three long centuries our constitution and our parliament functioned, dignified and unsullied, till the year 1380 when the treaty of Calmar united three kingdoms beneath one crown: Norway, Sweden, and Denmark, and Iceland became part of the united kingdoms—and it could be said that the flowering of Iceland ended there. The Danish kings, in their lust for power, ate up our independence a bite at a time and did all they could to control a people who had forgotten the confinement and indignity imposed by kings.

Perhaps it was this that made some of the difference between us. But then, we didn't even speak the same tongue as the Norsemen. So what more were they to us than the French or the Danes, the Germans or the Italians? Latter-day Saints? Yes, Latter-day Saints they were, but they weren't Icelandic. And they made it clear to us that we were not Norwegians.

But it didn't make that much difference, not on the trek. We found ways of getting along with each other. We made special friends of some, but not more than we seemed to from among the rest of the general company. And, after all, we were in the same boat together: We ferried the same swollen streams, used the same water spots, pulled our wagons over the same boulders, broke our wheels in the same potholes, cooked beside the same fires, divided the same stores of flour and buffalo meat.

I liked the taste of buffalo meat. I remembered Petur boasting in our small house by the warm peat fire of the great shaggy beasts that were bigger than oxen. I had never really believed I would ever see them. Yet here I was eating their flesh as a part of my diet, gathering dried buffalo chips for the fires—what strange things happen! What surprises life has in store!

As we left Nebraska, Petur's nineteenth birthday came. I nearly forgot it. Mother somehow contrived to bake cakes with sweet raisins in them. We drank to his health—cups of cool spring water. Petur marked the spot with a stake in the earth—pounded deep, with just a few inches showing upon which he had carved these words, both in English and Icelandic:

> Here Petur Jonsson, son of Iceland, marked
> the nineteenth anniversary of his birth
> in the year of our Lord 1857 on the twenty-
> third day of the month of July: Well in mind
> and spirit—Heading for Zion.

So like Petur! I had to smile.

We had also just passed the one-year mark: on the sixth day of June we had left Iceland. One whole year filled with so many difficult things to remember. One whole passing of season to season I had not seen: I had not fished the shallows with Petur, nor climbed the hanging cliffs, helped by Father's hand, to net the seafowl that flock to our headlands. I had not chased the puffins with my friend Halldor, nor played in Klettshellir, the Cave in the Cliff. Even buffalo steaks didn't taste like *rengi*—and I had not heard the sound of my grandfather's voice. . .

It was not so much the doing without; I could take that. There were plenty of new things to learn and see. It was the finality of it all, the *never again*, that haunted me and sent dreams to my sleep that disturbed me, so I would wake up tired, with very little appetite for the idea of traveling one day further into this alien land that was robbing me of my past and my future: and, of course, America had taken our Dena away.

But what to do? I had few choices. I was young, and youth has a way of wooing promise out of the most reluctant tomorrow, and seeing beauty where only barrenness meets the eye.

So we came at last to the Sweetwater River and we climbed Independence Rock with the others. *Sweetwater*—I liked that name. It amazed me that even here on a desert there should be so many sources of fresh, flowing water. We had no fresh water at home on our island. We would catch rainwater by placing barrels on our roofs and along certain high rocks. We were used to the taste of stale, tepid water. This cold, running water indeed tasted sweet.

We suffered the usual trials the Saints suffered in crossing the plains. Two men of our company died, and one was Icelandic. My father had known him well. He knelt by the graveside with tears streaming down his cheeks. I knew he was crying for the loss of the good man's life and for his widow, and for the children left fatherless in a strange land. But I knew he also cried for our Dena, and for a father who had watched the sea take two sons away, and for the son who was travel-weary and longing for home.

My mother did not cry. She took the widow and divided our small stores with her and fed her children and sat with the woman far into the night, and sent Father to mend her axle and gave her a kettle when one of hers bounced off the wagon and broke.

It seemed Mother was always doing something for someone. Quietly, with no fuss. When one of the women was about to give birth to a child, we'd find Mother missing. There were four babies born on that journey. Each one Mother assisted, helping to bring the new infant into the world, then rubbing the mother's back and bathing her body, mending her children's clothing and feeding them supper before turning back to our wagon and her own concerns. I watched her walk toward me after one birth; her dark eyes were glowing and a gentle expression softened the lines of her face. Perhaps what I wondered was written too stongly upon my own features.

"It helps me, Anna," she said, "don't worry. New life. A mother's happiness. That is good. I have had such happiness myself."

But her eyes misted over. And I had to look away from her eyes.

The time came when we reached Fort Bridger. Now the valley was scarcely more than a hundred miles away! I knew it, but I could not imagine. I had no solid pictures in my mind of what it would be. Elder Thorderson back home in Iceland had told us stories—but they were just stories, even to him. He had not ever seen the Valley. None of our people on this journey had.

"If we don't like it—we turn around and go straight back home!" Brother Palsson said that constantly near the end, his big laugh booming in echoes around us. I think each of us, in his own way, was a little afraid.

I remember the morning I saw the Valley. We had camped not far from the final descent. When I first awakened I felt a change in the air and all the faces around me seemed to reflect the play of a dozen emotions, the same excited apprehension I felt inside.

I was oblivious for once to dust and discomfort. When it came time and I had my turn to look down through the crevice, past the last sloping hills to the Valley floor, I took a breath and closed my eyes tight for a moment. When I opened them—while they focused—my first impression was of a vast wilderness shimmering wild and lovely before me. Then, straining my eyes, I could make out stretches of planted fields and fenced-off pasture dotted here and there with quiet herds. There were houses—not merely huts and cabins, as I had imagined. A real city, picture-book perfect, yet nearly swallowed by the emptiness upon which it sat—that sprawling expanse that spread on where the touch of man ended. Father pointed out the blue stretch of lake; I had nearly forgotten. Water! Perhaps there was fishing; perhaps there were gulls! Oh, for the sound of the waves, the wet smell of the air!

We knelt down right where we were and gave thanks to heaven. I felt the swell of gratitude in my heart—the sense of rightness, of benediction, with my father's hand firmly closed around mine. Peace, and a feeling that sang inside me. And often, since then, I've been glad for that moment—the strength of it has seen me through many a hard, hard time.

We sang for the first time that night in the Valley—for the very first time since we had left the island. With the loss of Dena we'd had little to sing for, and the emotions invoked by music were too sharp, too cruel—the emotions and the old memories, a hopeless blending. We cried as we sang, but the tears were good. We were home again—we were part of Zion, we were enclosed in the arms of God, and God would prevail.

We camped along the creek, repaired tools, washed clothing, blackened our worn, scuffed shoes and took stock of ourselves. Father and some of the brethren went to meet the prophet. I wanted so badly to go, too. But even Petur was not invited. Our first Sunday in the Valley we saw him, though.

There was a meeting in the bowery on Temple Square. Mother stayed with the young ones at camp. I walked through the city with Father on one side and Petur on the other. The air was warm and carried a sweet smell of growing things. The sky above was as blue as the sea back home. I gazed around me, content to take in all that was there—and then I saw him.

He was walking toward us with long, very powerful strides, in earnest conversation with the man who was walking beside him. I thought only, *I shall faint if he looks at me!* I must have subconsciously slowed my steps. I had time to notice that he wore a top hat of fine black silk and he carried a cane, an elaborate walking stick of some kind. Then he was upon us, and then, to my anguish—he stopped. I felt Petur poking my ribs. I raised my eyes slowly. As though waiting, waiting for *me*, his own eyes brightened. They were keen blue-gray and they met mine with an expression that drove all the fear from my mind and left me feeling warm, excited, and happy, all at the same time.

"Lovely morning, young sister," he said, and he touched his hat briefly. "Welcome to Zion."

His eyes shifted to meet my father's. He nodded kindly. But he was gone before the nod was complete, walking on past us. I stood still. I could *feel* his presence, the same way you can feel the sun on a cold spring morning when you walk into the pool of warmth from the chill of the shadows. I didn't want that warmth to dissolve away.

I watched after him: his head thrown back, sturdy broad shoulders. This was the man who had stood in Nauvoo and said to the Saints, "Here is Brigham. Have his knees ever faltered? Have his lips ever quivered?" This was the man who had seemed to speak and look like the murdered Joseph, so that the people listening thought it was their Prophet talking to them again. This was the man who had organized and led thousands of people over deserts and rivers, across mountains—in the face of death, disease, and Indians—here to this desert, and with his people built a city out of nothing. And this same man had paused in his grand, busy life, and had spoken to me!

Petur teased me, but Father knew how I felt at the honor. Even my mother paused when I told her of it and stared at me hard a moment.

"You get some paper," she said. "Write down what happened. Put the date on it, and if you can manage, put down how you felt."

"I can write in Icelandic how I felt," I told her.

She thought again. "Then do it," she told me. "But write the rest—all the rest that you can in the English, Anna."

I did just as she instructed, but I remember that it wasn't to please my mother I tried. I pretended that Brigham Young could see me, could read over my shoulder while I wrote. It made a great difference. I had never done so well with the English before.

We arrived in the City of the Saints sometime in late August. We stayed in tents along the stream, and while I helped Mother my brother Petur worked with the men and explored the city. Sina was a big girl of four who could take care of herself now. Gesli was six, into everything. Samuel was ten years old, and he was a good boy. He helped me sometimes with my chores, and he would often help Father, but with a quiet, detached little air, as though only half with us. I understood that; I could be the same way myself. But he worried me some. With a girl it's different. Boys should be more outgoing, sure-footed, able to take care of themselves, it seemed to me. So I worried about my brother Samuel, not knowing I was wasting my worrying on the wrong one.

Dena: for us she no longer existed. I never heard my mother utter her name, nor slip once and make any reference to her. Sometimes of a night Father sat by the fire, gazing, his eyes like glass, in his face a pain that the glassy eyes could not mask. Sometimes I would sit by him and he'd stroke my hair without saying a word, and we mourned in that quiet way together. Even after months, as it had been, when I'd hear a baby crying and fussing I'd feel myself turn, instinctively ready to help—and then I'd remember, and the hollow inside would start aching again. So we remained a family of five children, a father, and a mother—as whole, well, more so, than most of the families here.

The first week in September we packed our belongings again in the back of the wagon and drove past the houses and fields where the seagulls pecked at the brown, furrowed earth to the stretches of sagebrush, bound on the prophet's errand. Our Icelandic brethren had settled in a place called Spanish Fork, a settlement over the mountains and in the next valley. He sent us there for company of our own kind. He must have known what he was doing, but I wasn't happy to be leaving Salt Lake City and the gulls and the mountains and the Brethren behind. Spanish Fork had a strange ring to it. They said there was a freshwater lake on that side of the mountain, but we wouldn't be living right close to the lake, so there would be no smell of water in the wind, no sound of water to sleep and wake to, no wide expanse that whispered and breathed and was never still.

At a place called Point of the Mountain we paused to look back behind us. How wide the Valley was! A great, cavernous hole with the city carefully arranged like a child's toy blocks piled against one corner. But oh, how lovely the play of light and shadow across the quiet, checkered fields, the low brown foothills, the stretch of purple-gray mountains that circled it around!

"There's room here for a lot more Saints," said my practical mother. I agreed.

"I wish we could stay," I mumbled. "There's room for one small Icelandic family down there."

"Anna, Anna, will you never be happy? First you don't want to come to Salt Lake, then you don't want to leave. You must learn to be content with the present, Anna."

My father's hand came down on my shoulder. "Your mother is right. To make happiness wherever you are is a gift worth having."

Petur snorted. "I don't understand women. Always fussing over something. I think it's grand. A new valley of our own, with our own Icelanders—we can set things up just the way we like!"

I saw the look that crossed Father's face. It was gone in an instant. I couldn't quite read it, except I was sure he didn't think it would be as easy as Petur expected.

Chapter Five

Salt Lake City to me was Zion. It always would be. But Spanish Fork? I couldn't quite see it that way. I tried to. But perhaps my heart wasn't all in the trying.

It was a growing place, Spanish Fork, with several hundred Saints making homes there, both in and outside the fort that had been erected to protect the people during some recent Indian troubles. Petur was wild with disappointment to have missed the adventure. Chief Walker had died only a year before, and now an Indian farm was being constructed just a little west of the town. There were schoolhouses here—my mother pointed that out. Not one only, but two or three. I knew what that meant, though I tried to push the idea far out of my mind. Our people had settled along what was called the bench line in the southeast part of the settlement. We went there and found an abandoned dugout all ready for us. It was one room, very large, built half underground. The floor was packed earth, but the fireplace in the corner promised, at least, that we would not freeze that winter.

My mother is not one to sit still. Before we fell into our beds exhausted, all our boxes and trunks were unpacked, the things put away neatly, our quilts spread over the rawhide beds, our dishes safe in the cupboard, the pots by the fire, even pictures and trinkets from Iceland set up here and there.

I chose the smallest bed in the corner. The trundle beneath it that moved on small wooden rollers would have to do for both Gesli and little Sina. In the space beside me I spread a shawl and set out my own belongings: my comb and brush made of whalebone, three hair ribbons, the small hollowed-out box my grandfather had fashioned to hold the heavy brooches that used to belong to his mother, and now were mine. In a corner I propped my doll—my grandmother had made her, and the clothes she wore I had sewn myself. Last of all I brought out my books; I was the proud owner of three books of my very own. One of these contained the writings of an old, beloved Icelandic poet. It, too, had been in the family a very long time. I knew many of the poems by heart, and often at bedtime I would read one or two before saying my prayers. I wrote verses sometimes myself, though I showed them to no one. It was something deep in my blood, this longing to write—or to sing, as grandfather would say, and put words to the singing which came naturally from the heart of our people.

That first night before going to bed I took little Sina and warned her to leave my treasures alone. I told her if she would be good and not touch them she might play with the doll in the corner. She was glad to agree. With her finger in her mouth she took courage to ask me if she could sleep with the doll that night. She had lost her own doll when we had forded a swollen creek. I tucked her in and pressed the precious bundle in with her.

"I think she'll be glad to have someone to sleep with, Sina," I told her. "She's a little frightened to sleep her first night here alone." I'd had my doll since I was little—as little as Dena. In fact, I had often let the baby hold it, or bounced it in front of her, making her laugh.

"What's your dolly's name?" Sina asked.

"You know it. She's named Hela, after our grandmother."

"Did she die?"

"Yes, she died before you were born. She was very lovely—as pretty as you and me put together, and twice as nice!"

I thought Sina might giggle at that, but her round face was solemn.

"If she were my doll," she said in a small voice, "I'd call her Dena."

A cold chill, like the ice-rain back home, crawled along my skin. I resisted an impulse to kneel and hold her.

"You may call her Dena if you want. I think she'd like that. And I don't believe Grandmother would mind at all."

I planted a kiss on her cheek. "Go to sleep now, darling." Then I crawled into bed myself, feeling grateful that my mother had worn me out. I wanted to sleep. I desperately wanted to sleep, and stop feeling.

Our very first day in Spanish Fork there were two things that happened. One I looked upon as good; one I thought was bad. But both had a mixing of threads in them that were hidden to me at the moment. How blind we are, with a flat, straight-ahead, very narrow vision, missing light and color and depth, seeing only the image stamped on the surface, and little more.

The good thing happened first. Right after breakfast, before we washed the dishes, my father said, "I think Anna needs to sit down for a moment. Right over there in that chair."

There was only one chair, a rocker with two broken spindles. The table where we ate had a long bench on either side. I stifled a smile. What did my father have in mind? I sat in the rocker.

"This is an important day for us all, but especially for Anna." My father cleared his throat. Little Sina drew closer. "This is our first day in our new home," Father continued. "In the years to come we'll remember this day and celebrate it with joy. And to help us remember, we'll celebrate Anna's birthday as well."

"Look at her face!" Petur pointed to me and laughed, but the laugh was a kind one. Father knew I had forgotten! His own eyes smiled. Mother handed me a package—and then another. Presents! I opened the little one first. It was a paper with a peppermint stick and half a dozen horehound pieces wrapped in it.

"For your sweet tooth," Samuel said. "They're from me and Petur."

I wanted to hug him. "How?" I asked. Petur was anxious.

"We worked while we were in Salt Lake, remember. We bought them ourselves, kept them hidden all this time."

I unwrapped the next one and saw, through a blur, lying there on my apron, a copybook of my own with a new wooden pencil, shiny and unsharpened. I rubbed my eyes. I put the pencil up to my nose and smelled of the wood. I had never owned such a treasure as this in my life!

How? my eyes asked again, as I looked at my father. He smiled. "There are ways," he said. "Use it wisely, daughter."

"Huh! Wisely," my mother grumbled. "I'll get no work from her!" That was her way of teasing. I knew by the tone of her voice.

"Anna's work today is not washing the dishes. Our Sina must learn to help Mother more now."

Something started to close hard and tight inside me.

"What do you mean, Father?"

He smiled at me kindly. "You know now, Anna. It is to the school with you and Petur, and Samuel, too."

"I'm too old for school," Petur snorted. "There's work to be done. You could use me and Samuel, and ten more hands!"

"I know that, son, but the work will be here. Work's always with us. The man who has knowledge can choose the work he will do. I want that for you, Petur."

I rose. I tried to smile. I kissed Father gently. "I'll try to do well for you, Father." I knew what a sacrifice it would be for him to pay for our education—and I knew he counted it more important than the food we ate or the clothes on our backs. He had felt that way back home in Iceland; he felt it even more strongly here, where education would equip us to succeed and be productive in a new, different world.

I hugged Mother then and whispered a thank you into her ear. She fussed me from her.

"You'd better hurry, be off with you, now! There'll be work in plenty for you to do when you get back home."

I took my new treasures to my own corner. Sina followed. "Be a good girl today and help Mother, and when I get home from school I will give you a horehound. If you suck it slowly it will last you most of the evening."

She nodded, her eyes bright with sparkles, like sea spray in the morning. "I'll be good, I promise!" she cried.

I wanted to leave the copybook there. I was frightened to take it, unsure what the school would be like, not wanting it hurt, or scuffed—or even looked at by others. But then, how nice it would be to go armed with something—something new, something all my own. I took it with me and walked out into the bright sunshine where Petur waited.

"Samuel's already started down; come on, Anna," he cried. He grabbed my free hand and tugged me along with him. "I only have to go to school half day," he boasted. "Then I'm free to work with the men."

I said nothing. What could I say except what I felt inside: *I'm afraid. I'm too old and awkward. I don't like strangers. I don't want to learn about America and American things.* I couldn't say any of that to Petur. He would call me a baby. I was—but I didn't want to hear Petur say so. We caught up with Samuel.

"How old are you?" he asked, without looking at me, without even breaking his stride.

"I'm eighteen. I'm a woman now—so what am I doing going off to school with a couple of overgrown boys like you?"

I said it. I hadn't meant to say it. Petur roared. "You were always a bit of a scaredy-cat, Anna."

I pulled my hand away from his, but he grabbed it again. "That's all right," he said under his breath. "I'm scared myself. I'll take care of you, Anna. Isn't that what big brothers are for?"

It didn't seem to me Petur kept his word. The teacher assigned us seats right next to each other, in a section of young people our age and size. There were thirty, maybe as many as forty pupils, reciting lessons, asking questions. I strained to listen, but I missed many of their words, they all talked so fast. I turned to Petur a time or two to ask him a question—in Icelandic. But he only shook his head and set his lips.

"Speak the English, Anna."

I turned away, tears stinging my eyes. Then, forgetting, I would speak to him, all anxious again.

"Speak English, Anna. I promised Mama I'd only speak English with you."

So it was Mother behind it! I should have known that. I turned my back to him, feeling so alone that I went all weak inside. The teacher gave me a book to look at and copy: a primer, it said, for small children, I'm sure—at least the pictures seemed to be drawn for children and the words were simple and printed large. She walked over beside me and bent down till her head was even with mine.

"That's a lovely book you have there," she said, touching my present. "I wouldn't want to spoil it with early practice. Use this while you're starting to learn."

I thanked her, happy to have the crude slate to practice on. I slipped my book down onto my lap and started to copy the letters of the English alphabet: A—B—C—A CAT—A RAT—THE CAT AND THE RAT RAN—CAN ANN FIND THE CAT? The teacher bent over. She had been watching me while I worked. She added an A so the sentence read: CAN ANNA FIND THE CAT?

"That's your name," she said. "A lovely name, Anna." She patted me lightly, her hand cool against my arm. She moved forward to work with the boy just in front of me. She *glided* forward, her movements so graceful—her voice so sweet, her smile so kind and sincere. I thought fiercely to myself: *I want to be like her! I can do it. Father says I'm pretty! I must learn to read, that's the first step. And I can copy the way she walks, how she moves her hand, the way she brushes back her hair—I know I can! I won't be different! I won't be laughed at any longer!*

It was a brave resolve, and my heart meant it. We had been laughed at, after all, since we left Iceland. Laughed at in Liverpool, on the ship, in the city of Philadelphia, on the Iowa plain. When I slid into my seat that morning a little girl with a bright yellow braid whispered to her neighbor, then pointed to me, and they both laughed. I had known, of course; it was bound to happen. I still wore the old, homemade shoes—my father had made them. Both my stockings and dress were wool, and the cut was different —and then there was the kerchief I wore and the cap on my head. But I wasn't something ugly—something to laugh at! I thought my way of dressing much prettier, really, than theirs. I resented the fact that different meant inferior, even here—even in Spanish Fork, which they told me was Zion.

The lessons were bearable; the lessons passed quickly. I am not a particularly quick learner, but I can memorize anything, even in English. And the teacher—thanks to the teacher, the sting was gone.

Nevertheless, when at last she smiled and dismissed us, the feeling of release was intense and sweet. Petur had left earlier as he had predicted. I went to find Samuel, eager to shake the dust of the place off my feet, to run all the long way home. I found him. He was surrounded by a group of rough, unkempt, surly boys. They were poking their fingers at him and laughing. I pushed my way through the group. When he saw me, he called out in Icelandic. The laughter increased. One of the boys with a broad, freckled face shouted, "What kind of gibberish is this, boys? He sounds like a monkey."

They all roared. The freckled boy spat right at Samuel's feet. I shoved him aside with my shoulder and grabbed Samuel's hand.

But in the scuffle, as Samuel moved to match my steps, the boy stuck out his leg. Samuel tripped and fell very hard on his stomach. His nose hit the packed clay earth and it started to bleed. I lifted him up. He was fighting the tears, but he smiled at me bravely. I was speaking to him in our own language without even knowing. The boys around us continued their crude banter, but I hardly heard their words. They were bigger than Samuel—most of them looked closer to my age. I turned on them with what words I had.

"Shame on you! You laugh to pick on a child. Go away."

I took my handkerchief out of my pocket and gave it to Samuel. Together we walked through the ring of boys. Short and stocky, most of them were, and as far as speaking was concerned, they sounded funny themselves. Their words didn't make the same sounds at all as the teacher's. But they were English words, all the same, and that made the difference.

We didn't run home. We walked sedately—on purpose. I would have died before letting those louts back there think us afraid. Two or three of them followed for a way, loath to give up their taunting.

"They're going on up the hill—you're right, Huw. Must be some of them queer Norwegians."

Norwegians! Something in me bristled. There were two things that pestered my thoughts the whole way home: One, I would learn the English and learn it quickly—and speak better than anyone else in the school. It would be a tool I could use against them, a way to prove I was as good as anyone else. But the second thought was this: I was proud to be different. I wouldn't change what I was for the likes of them! I was Icelandic, and I would remain Icelandic, school or no school, Zion or no Zion.

One last thought pestered my mind as I reached the dugout. Petur had said, "I'll take care of you, Anna." But he hadn't been there when I needed him. Life was like that. At the bad times it seemed you were always left standing alone. I had better remember that. There was no one to count on—no one but the person you found when you looked inside.

Petur was still off working with Father when Samuel and I got home. We said nothing to Mother about what had happened, but pitched in hanging clean clothes and fixing the meal. I couldn't get used to the differences in what we ate here, though some of it was much better than food at home.

Over the table later that evening I found myself hungry—studying seemed to work up an appetite. We had new bread Mother had baked that morning and potatoes cooked in their jackets and a few fresh greens, and a gravy thick with chunks of meat. Father poured it over his potatoes, then over his bread. He seemed hungry, too, but his eyes were happy. The men he worked with were men he had known back home—some of them friends from childhood. They talked together, not worrying, as their children had to, if they lapsed into Icelandic. And Father had discovered that there would be work to do.

He could build anything with his hands, my father. He was skilled in the use of iron as well as wood. And here there were things to be built in plenty: bridges, homes, a public storehouse—a certain brother had already approached him concerning work in constructing a mill. It made me feel better, seeing my father happy. And Petur! He was a mile high. They were letting him drive one of the wagons to bring the supplies in and haul out the debris and large stones. He was one of the men now. He had only one foot in our world—his mornings at school. And he was tugging hard to dislodge that.

"They could work me twelve hours a day," he argued. "You know that."

Father nodded. "You haven't twelve hours to give. They will take what you have to give, Petur."

"I can finish my lessons by eleven, I know I can, Father. That way I can catch the earlier wagon and gain a whole hour—"

The discussion went around and around. I stopped listening. Petur would get his way in the end. He was like that. He never gave up. He could wear anybody down. Later, when he asked me how school went, I told him only the things he wanted to hear. He smiled and nodded.

"See, Anna," he said, "our mother was right. Things will work out for us all. You'll see that."

Let him believe it, I said to myself. I found Sina and gave her the promised horehound, enjoying the look of pleasure that lighted her eyes. Samuel was down by the stream drawing water—fresh water, that endless miracle here! When he came in the door, his hands loaded, I popped a horehound into his mouth. He frowned a little.

"You didn't have to do that, Anna. We meant them for you."

I kissed his cheek, though he squirmed away. "Well, Samuel, if they're mine I can do what I like with them, right?" He nodded with reluctance, but his eyes showed pleasure.

I noticed Gesli watching me closely. I called him over. Poor Gesli, betwixt and between. No longer a baby, but not big enough yet for school. I gave him his candy.

"Did you think I'd forget you, Gesli?" I rubbed his head. He snuggled against me a moment, then ran off, contented. I was tired, but there was one thing left to do.

I slipped outside. The sky was darkening; the mountains formed a jagged contour of peaks against strips of pale pink. I watched while the pink washed to gray and the slender rock outline, sharply etched against the dim sky, became vague, indistinct.

I drew out my book and opened it. The white pages were clean and unmarked yet. They seemed to cry out for the shape of firm, lovely letters upon them, the beauty of a captured emotion, a clear, ringing thought preserved forever upon that slim surface. My fingers were itching. My mind seethed and surged. I would write a poem. I had written many poems in Iceland. The sound of the sea, the call of the birds just above my head, a storm on the ocean, a black crag wet with spray and half hidden by mist—countless things on my island to stir the imagination.

I gazed at the fading beauty before me and struggled with words that did not fit the shape of my eager feelings. Zion—I could write about Zion. But oh, those thoughts were teeming with contradictions! I turned back to beauty. Beauty is beauty, whatever the tongue. But the words as I wrote them in English were halting and clumsy—they didn't fit right or fall right, or sound right at all. At last I scribbled them out, my new page ruined—and my new resolves ruined with it. I stomped back inside. Learn the English! Walk like the teacher, Miss Fletcher! Impossible. Why should I even attempt it—make a fool of myself with trying?

I slunk into bed, my eyes aching with held-back tears. But then the words came! Delightful words in the forbidden language, words to paint my loved, lost home, to capture the feel of the air in the morning and the singing sigh of the sea as she swallowed the sun and then murmured lullabies to herself through the quiet dark hours.

I stumbled out of bed and reached for my tablet, then tiptoed to where the fire still throbbed and glowed. I stirred the embers a little and started writing. I don't know if my parents saw me. No one said a word. I lost track of the time as I wrote, and the chill that crept through me meant nothing to my spirit that struggled and soared, and at last fluttered down, settled back in my body, and gave in to the needs of comfort and sleep. The words I had written were good words. I would sleep well now—and I would not try to write verses in English again. My own tongue had words that sang, that served every feeling that cried forth from the human heart. I would not betray them, nor forget their ancient beauty.

No, from now on, when I wrote, I would write in the language I loved.

Chapter Six

The next day in school proved little better. The scruffy boys waited till lunchtime when Petur was gone to begin pestering Samuel again. But I stuck close to him, even though that increased their taunts to a feverish pitch. On the walk home Samuel addressed the issue in his straightforward manner, so reasonable for a boy his age.

"You make it worse by trying to help, Anna. I'll be all right— I can manage for a while. I'll get Petur to teach me to fight, and then when I'm ready, I'll knock their teeth right out of their heads."

I was tempted to smile, though this really was far from a smiling matter. "You think that will work? What they want is to fight, Samuel. You fight them once and they'll keep on fighting, and it will be a matter of which is the next to get even! Besides, you'd have to sink pretty far down to reach their level. There must be other ways."

Samuel shook his head. "You speak to them in their own language. That's how you gain their respect."

Where had Samuel picked that up? The poor sweetheart. I couldn't see him learning to fight, or holding his own in the ruthless give-and-take such scrapping required.

We were lucky for a day or two: it rained buckets. Miss Fletcher kept us inside the building and her watchful eye quelled even the thought of rebellion. After school was dismissed we two set out quickly, and I don't think even those boys had much heart for a fight with mud seeping through their shoes and rain soaking their backs.

So we two made it, by the skin of our teeth, one day at a time. But everyone else in the family, as Petur had predicted, seemed to ease into life in Zion with no trouble at all. Even Brother Palsson, for all his fussing, seemed content to accept conditions here.

In September, around the same time we arrived in the valley, the local sisters had organized a branch of Relief Society, which had been established by the Prophet Joseph himself in Nauvoo, with his wife, Emma, as the first president. I knew that because the missionary in Iceland had told us stories of the beginnings of the Church. I enjoyed his stories—almost as much as I did his voice and his smile, and the sensation of being near him. Oh, how I missed him sometimes!

The Relief Society went well in our city. Over fifty women were members, my mother one. She sewed and cooked and cared for the sick, and helped in childbirth, her healing skills quickly recognized by others. My mother never ceased to amaze me— and puzzle me, too. I'd have given a fortune to know what thoughts hid behind her calm features, what feelings seethed in her quiet heart. Nothing seemed to upset or disturb her, to eat through that calm, everlasting resolve to keep going! It didn't matter to her that some of the ladies shunned her. She went to the meetings and served the local families as freely as those from Iceland. She spoke to the women, unmindful of or at least unbothered by slowness of tongue, by words that wouldn't come, by mistakes in grammar. Was she happy? I didn't know, and I couldn't tell. Sometimes I thought to myself, *If being happy means being like Mother, I'd rather be miserable like myself for the rest of my life.*

Petur's days went quickly and so did Father's, working long hours, then coming home to do what jobs and chores we women could not handle. Father did little things as well. He mended the rocker and built another chair so that he and Mother could sit together of an evening when we children were in bed. He put a new sod roof on the dugout, against the coming of winter, and built a shelf for Mother to place her small treasures upon. His hands seemed never idle; even late by the fire he would whittle away at some toy for the children while Mother did mending or worked on a piece of stitchery. And if sometimes I saw sadness in his eyes and that faraway look, his face usually wore a peaceful, contented expression.

There was work to do in plenty, so the days passed quickly, and I kept my own aching heart to myself. I had found one thing at the school which I could excel in: spelling. I could memorize the words quickly and not forget them. It irked the girls to see me pass to the head of the line, sending them all back to their seats with heads hanging. One time I outspelled everyone in the room, boys and girls alike, and one of the scrappers—the boys who were bothering Samuel—shouted out loud, "Bully for the girl from Iceland!" I looked up, dumbfounded. He stood grinning, his round face as chock-full of mischief as ever. But the light in his eyes seemed friendly, not mocking. Blue eyes, deep as the sea back home.

On Sundays, we met in the house of a brother—an Icelandic brother. We read from the scriptures, heard sermons preached, sang Icelandic songs and songs from the Latter-day Saint hymnbook. Some of the hymns were lovely; I truly enjoyed them, drawn by the music to feel the words. But when it came to our own songs, I sang my heart out. Music to me was an outlet, like the writing of words—an expression of something within me beyond expression, and comfort to what was otherwise comfortless.

The years 1856 and 1857 were known as the Reformation years. Some of the Saints had grown lax, some independent during the Nauvoo persecutions and the long trek west. This was a time of searching souls, of casting out evil—from our actions to one another, and from the heart. The people were constantly being exhorted to true repentance, and the pure principles of the gospel urged and retaught. My father thought it was a good thing. When I asked him about it, he scratched his head a moment to give himself time to reply.

"It's a constant struggle, Anna, a constant struggle."

"What is a constant struggle?"

He stopped his work, took a moment to gather the nails that were scattered around him. "The purpose of earth life is to learn to govern ourselves, to subdue the natural man and develop within us the qualities of the heavenly parents we left behind."

I knew that. But he was off track a little. I was digging for something else. I persisted. "Aren't we taught that all men are the same in God's eyes—or at least all Saints?"

His eyes widened at that. I think he knew at last where my thoughts were leading.

"Are we all Saints, or are some Saints worth more than others? What good does it do to purge yourself if you pass a Saint from Iceland on the pathway and lower your eyes and can't stand to say even hello?"

His eyes grew dark and he shook his head. "Now, Anna—"

"I mean it, Father. The Saints here don't even want us going to meeting with them."

"That's not true, daughter." His voice had grown suddenly stern. "It is as much our own fault as any other's. We are frightened, we cling to our old ways. We feel secure in learning the gospel along with each other. Time—it takes time and patience, Anna . . ."

He shook his head again, as though suddenly tired. Then he drew me to him, with his hand on my shoulder.

"Look over there."

I looked where his finger pointed. The ring of mountains, furrowed and craggy, stretched clear around in a wide, graceful arc to Mt. Timpanogos—past Provo, to Battle Creek, many miles by the road, yet here in magnificence, spread for my eyes to see.

"How long do you think it took to create those mountains?"

I squirmed a little. "A long time. A long time, even for God."

"That's right, girl. To create an eternal soul—godlike and shining, free and powerful. How long would you say?"

How well my father knew me! "I'd have to say a bit longer than a quick year of Reformation."

He hugged me to him. "Anna, my Anna. You mustn't judge, it is not good. It makes you no better than the worst of the faults you observe in others. There are Saints from all parts of the world gathered in our little community, remember. We all bring our ways—our fears, our preferences—with us. The gospel hasn't had time to temper us yet, to unite us truly as brothers and sisters. Give us some time—some time and faith, my Anna."

I knew he was right. I closed my eyes. "But I'm homesick, Father, and sometimes I'm so lonely. And everything here is a struggle—"

"I know . . . I know . . ." His voice was as soft as snow falling on water. "Be careful not to confuse things, Anna. Your sorrows are not the fault of these people here. Don't punish them, daughter, for what you suffer."

I hadn't meant to cry, but his arms were around me and it was easy to hide my face against his strong chest. He stroked my hair with his gentle fingers.

"There, there, a cry will be good for you."

"I'm a baby, like Petur says," I mumbled. He held me from him so he could look into my face.

"A baby! You must not listen to Petur. You are a courageous young woman, Anna, and beautiful, too."

I dropped my eyes before his. "It is true, my daughter. You look more and more like my mother each day."

On sudden impulse I hugged him tightly. "Oh, Father! I would be hopeless without you."

He seemed to tremble at my words. "That is what I am here for. Father . . . daughter . . . we all help each other along."

I went into the house feeling light and unburdened. But my father sat on the bench with his work undone. He sat there, staring ahead, till we called him to supper, and though he smiled and teased with the children, his eyes were sad. It was I who, proud and persistent, had torn the cover from his own store of sorrow, carefully guarded and concealed in his heart.

*Father . . . daughter . . . we all help each other—*I gave him an extra kiss before going to bed. It was no help to call up his pain, to make him suffer. I would do better in the future—be brave like him. Cry alone, where my tears had no power to hurt him. It was a promise I made myself—but so hard to keep in the unkind days that waited around the corner.

Chapter Seven

The days grew colder. The greedy darkness nibbled at the afternoon hours. We did both our morning chores and our evening chores in shadow and when we walked to school our breath froze in trails through the air.

I kept waiting for the snow, but only more rain came. The bright autumn colors faded to the dull shades of the mud we walked in. Only the furthest mountain peaks had a white icing on them. The valleys were merely soggy and dreary.

I continued to go to school and did well in my studies and fit the pattern which seemed expected of me: sit with the Icelandic students, be friendly with them, but not in your native tongue, and smile at the other students only if you're first smiled at; speak only if you're first spoken to. Samuel made his own way as well. He had several friends now. There were no girls from Iceland my own age. I helped the younger ones as much as I could, but I longed for Halldor and the games we'd played and the talks we'd had, and the safe, girlish world I had left behind.

One day Petur came home from work early. I had a sore throat and had stayed home from school myself. He got his rifle out from the chest at the back of the dugout. It was one of those days they call Indian summer, when a sun as hot as August has dried up the mud and the bees, confused, poke about for flowers, and a golden light coats the fields and the smell of ripe pumpkins is mixed with the sweet, lazy scent of the last fall roses. I felt languid and warm with the day. I followed Petur. "Are you going to shoot squirrels?" I asked. Perhaps I could go with him.

He shook his head. "Not squirrels, exactly." He kept on loading, his head bent over his task.

"Then what?"

At my question Mother looked up from her work in the kitchen.

"There may be trouble at the Indian farm."

"What kind of trouble?" I felt my heart leap. There had been no Indian battles since we had been here. I knew that the agent at the Indian farm west of town, Dr. Hurt, was not friendly toward the Mormons. But what real trouble could there be?

Petur, through with his loading, took up his rifle and the pouch beside it and walked to the door.

"I'm not sure, Anna. Rumor has it that Hurt and a bunch of Peteetneet's warriors are on the warpath."

I must have gasped. He kissed Mother's cheek and grinned over at me. "I don't know, it may not be true, Anna. But since they've called us out to help, you can bet I'm going."

"Where's Father?"

Petur shook his head. "He stayed at the workings. Some of the men don't think it will come to blows. Father said he hadn't much interest in those kinds of doings—"

My mother nodded, as though well pleased.

"Be careful, Petur."

He grinned and nodded, and then he was gone. I said to my mother, "He wanted to go. Did you see his eyes?"

"He is like my father. You and I can't see it, Anna. But to some men danger is sauce to the meat, an excitement in their blood like intoxication. Would you peel the potatoes, please?"

I peeled the potatoes, and tried to forget the expression in Petur's eyes.

Father came home late. He knew very little. We piled a plate with food for Petur and set it aside. The children were long in bed when I heard him coming. I met him at the door. "What happened, Petur?"

He brushed past me, sat down in the far corner, and started cleaning his gun.

"There's food Mother saved for you. Would you like to eat now?" He shook his head. "Please tell me what happened, Petur."

"Hurt's riled up Peteetneet's warriors, all right." He didn't look up from his work and his voice was shaded. "The brethren almost had Hurt in their hands, but he slipped away. They figure he's headed to find Sidney Johnston's men."

"Johnston's Army?" Something went cold inside me. "They'll tell lies about us, Petur—"

"It won't much matter. Johnston has come all the way out here on the strength of a pack of lies. A few more won't even be noticed."

His voice sounded tired. I tried to picture the Indians, supple as shadows, merging noiselessly at the mouth of the canyon, their war paint gleaming, led by a hard-faced white man.

"Then there wasn't trouble? No shooting, no—"

There was a knock at the door. A loud, pounding kind of knock. Petur rose from his chair.

"That will be for me, Father," he said. I looked at my father who went quietly to the door and stood beside Petur.

"Mr. Jonsson?" The man who spoke looked right past Petur. I felt Petur's body tense. My father nodded.

"I am Einar Jonsson, yes. What may I do to help you?"

My father indicated with his arm for the man to step inside. He didn't seem to notice the gesture. He coughed into his hands.

"I'm Bishop Evans—Jonathan Evans. And I'm here on a little matter to do with your son."

My father's eyebrows shot up in an arch, but his face remained quiet. My mother's knitting needles went still in her hands.

"Please step inside."

"There's no need, brother. I've come in the interest of a couple of fathers who are pretty riled." The man tried to laugh, and the sound was friendly. "I thought it better for me to come."

"And these other men? Who are they? And what have they against my son?"

The bishop coughed again. "It seems your son here got in a fight with two or three other lads—the Pritchard boy, Huw Jones

—I'm not sure of the others. They're younger than your boy, and he caused some damage. Busted a tooth and broke Davey Pritchard's nose—"

"And their fathers are angry with Petur?"

"Well, you know how that is. They say he's a bully, they say . . ." The bishop paused, shook his head as though trying to wrest something from it. "These things blow over. But they want an apology, feel your son owes it to them—"

Father turned to Petur, slowly, with wide, sad eyes. "What happened, Petur?"

Petur looked him straight in the face. "Sir, the boys were too young to be there. They were playing hooky from school and everyone knew it. Brother Miller told me to go over and send them back. That's all I did, but they wouldn't let it rest there."

"What do you mean?" my father urged. Bishop Evans stepped closer, one foot nearly inside the door.

Petur shrugged his shoulders. "The usual taunts about how I talk and where I come from. Then one of them said a word about Samuel—a nasty word, and the others laughed. I knew then that they were the ones who had given him trouble. I told him to take back the word or he'd wish he had."

I watched the muscles in my father's jaw tighten. Bishop Evans looked down at his feet.

"He wouldn't. So I said, 'I'll take you on all at once, boys. That ought to be fair.'" Petur made a noise in his throat. "They were quite a bunch of scrappers, I'll tell you. I bit off a sizeable hunk—"

His fingers went unconsciously up to his eye. It was swollen black and yellow. I hadn't noticed. That was why he had walked quickly by me and sat in the corner.

"How many boys were there, Petur?"

"Five, Father. All of them Welsh."

My father's eyes flashed. "That doesn't matter."

"It matters, Father. They're the boys who've tormented Samuel since school began. Even Anna—ask Anna to tell you, Father."

"Anna has nothing to do with what happened today, Petur." My father took a deep, audible breath. "Did you fight all five of these boys?"

"No, I didn't. Only four. There was one boy who wouldn't fight. Said the odds were stacked as it was. But near the end there he jumped on my back to pull me off—that's about all, sir—"

"That'd be Owen," the bishop said. "Owen Davies. Sounds like something Owen would do—"

"Well, Petur." My father put his hand on Petur's arm. "We'll settle for four, then. If Bishop Evans here will be kind enough to escort you, you will go right now to the homes of these boys—"

"Now, perhaps that's hasty. I hadn't heard your son's side of the story before."

"There is no other side of the story, friend. Petur was acting under orders. A regular soldier would be severely disciplined for that kind of breach of discipline."

Petur stepped backward. Something in my father's voice made it painful to hear.

"I'll go, sir. Heaven knows I don't owe it to them—" There was pain in his voice as well. "But I'll go for your sake."

My father's fingers tightened against Petur's flesh. "For my sake? It is not my honor at stake here, Petur, but yours! You must go for the sake of your own honor."

Petur swallowed. His face was dark. "I will go, sir."

He turned and walked into the night. The bishop stood there until my father found words to release him.

"I thank you for coming—as a friend, as a brother, for giving us this chance to make things right."

The bishop reached out for my father's hand. "It's a pleasure. A pleasure to make your acquaintance, Brother Jonsson, I mean—"

They parted. The bishop followed Petur into the night where my aching eyes could not follow. Father shut and bolted the door and went back to his seat by the fire. He took my mother's hands in his and rubbed them gently.

"Time for bed, Anna, don't you think?"

"May I wait up for Petur?"

"He will be a while. I don't think so, Anna."

I wanted to plead, but I knew it would do me no good. I walked back to the end of the room and got ready for bed. I said my prayers, and that seemed to help a little. I lay in bed and thought about Petur and the hostility he would face. I had another thought, too, for my mind to examine. "There was one boy," Petur had said, "who wouldn't fight me—thought the odds were already stacked—"

Owen Davies. The bishop had said the name almost instantly. "Sounds like something Owen would do—"

I closed my eyes. I could see his face. "Bully for the girl from Iceland!" He had said that. He had also picked up my books for me when I had dropped them one day last week. He had the bluest, bluest eyes!

I blinked out his image and tried hard to think about Petur, to share his pain and the loneliness he must feel among unkind strangers.

Chapter Eight

The week before Christmas the first snow fell, at least the first snow on the valley floor. Living up on the bench line as we did, we got more than some others. It was a light, fluffy snow and it melted quickly—the sun burned it off right before our eyes. Higher up its depth defied the sun's powers, so the mountains stayed clean and white. Petur assured me that there would be more on the ground before Christmas. Mother laughed at me. "Do you like wet feet and red noses, Anna? It is nice, the sunny mornings, the mild, still nights."

"You don't miss the snow?"

"I don't miss the wind and the ice and the glare of white, everywhere white—"

"Well, I do. I feel sorry for the earth, all brown and ugly. The snow covers up the dead spots until spring comes to change them. I can't wait for more snow to fall."

The day before Christmas it snowed again. But this snow was heavy and cold and it piled up quickly. We finished our last-minute baking. It seemed to me we had spent every spare moment for the past six weeks in baking. My good dress already felt tight at the middle, for I was never one to resist sweets. Many of the cookies and cakes we made were of Norwegian origin, different from the fare we had known on our island. A nice blending of Latter-day Saint Americanism with the culture of her ancestors —that was my mother. It was as though Iceland no longer existed for her. She could adjust, she could make this place home as surely as the rockbound spot of land in that far northern sea.

Mother had contrived an adapted form of *skyr*, but there was no *rengi*, cod, or halibut to be eaten. We made do with sausages, lamb cutlets, black bread, cheese, and Brigham tea, a harmless concoction of herbs that, if not satisfying, at least was beneficial to body and brain. Of course, we all missed our Icelandic coffee; and, of course, no one ever said so out loud. It was one of the things we had put behind us forever, and one, after all, of the least to be missed.

When dusk fell Father built up a lovely fire. We ate by its light, hardly needing candles. We used the old carved bowls and plates we had brought along with us, some fashioned by hands long frozen in death—one carved for my mother by my father on the day of their wedding, one carved for the day their first child was born. When we bowed our heads for the blessing on the food I was surprised to hear my father speak the words in Icelandic. How warm, how gentle those sounds on my ear!

Later, when we all sat around the fire, Father brought out his *langspil*, an instrument much like a fiddle but with only two strings. We sang the old Icelandic songs till our voices grew drowsy. Then we took out the family Bible and, in Icelandic, read about the birth of the Savior of man. The snow outside fell more softly, piling higher and higher. Long ago, in the year 1000 A.D. the *Althing* voted to make our land Christian. There were reasons beyond the spiritual for their decision, and the old gods put up a struggle and would not die easily to convenience a mortal's will. Though no blood was spilt, many hearts were broken. One god made no room for the spirits of Odin and Thor and Frigga. My father felt that in doctrine regarding the supreme God Mormonism was close in form and spirit to the ancient religion of our people. For us there was always the unknown god of legend. Even Odin himself, the Allfather, bowed in homage before this mightiest god. As Mormons we bowed to the great God, too. But we knew Him, knew His name, our relationship to Him, felt His Spirit through the words He had given His people.

So the last thing we did that night was read in the English, from the book the Saints called the Book of Mormon, the Nephite account of the events at Christ's birth on this far continent where we were living. Some of the old Nephite names sounded warmer to me than the tones of the English. When we were finished we sat by the fire together and prayed an English prayer. Then we went to bed and waited for Christmas to come to our little valley.

Christmas morning we ate a *dagmal* of bread and cheese, milk and warm pancakes, then opened the gifts we had fashioned for one another. I remember the fine new apron my mother gave me and the wooden doll Father made for Sina, dressed to match her own Sunday best, thanks to Mother's deft fingers and conservative ways. I remember little else, for one thing overshadowed, overwhelmed the rest of the day.

There were no paths cut through the deep drifts of snow where the roads went. But that was no concern; we were happy inside with food, companionship, and an ample fire. Father and Petur had cared for the animals early that morning. There was little in all the long day to demand our time. But Samuel and Gesli were eager to try their new presents—ice skates Father had made the old way from the shinbone of a cow. So Mother gave in to their pleas and they bundled up warmly and headed out to see what fun they could find.

A few moments later we all heard a terrible shouting, then a crash and a hearty laugh. Father threw the door open and his anxious face softened into lines of pleasure. Piled up in the snow before us were Samuel and Gesli and a young man with flailing arms and long legs and a hat on top of his head that had seen some wearing, and eyes as blue as sea water—face and eyes and voice of sea and island, of rocks and gulls, of *home!* I flew through the door and found myself out in the snow with his arms about me, laughing with him. And Mother did not even scold when we left puddles on her floor and a pile of wet clothing.

The confusion moved somehow into the space by the fire, and we all found spots to sit down, and the layers of talking—voice on top of voice, stumbling over each other—evened into a pattern where sense could emerge. Elder Thorderson sipped at the mug of hot drink Mother gave him, cupping the warmth in both his hands. And we tempered our questions, asking only one at a time, and waiting for his answers.

He had been in the Salt Lake Valley for several days—yes, it had been a good trip over. No troubles, not even a death; the Lord had blessed them. He had found a last-minute ride to our valley, arriving late in the night, putting up with Brother Palsson. He looked over at me and winked.

"I've missed all of you. Are you happy to see me, my little Anna?"

I blushed and looked down at the floor, but his words had pleased me—the attention, the "my little Anna"—

The questions went on. What had the people thought when we left? He told all the stories: excitement for a day or two, a high vein of resentment, but no violence, thank the Lord. He told of the weather, the crops, the sheep, the success of the fishing. At last I said, rather loudly, "And what of Grandfather?"

The whole room seemed to hold its breath. "Is he well?"

Elder Thorderson nodded slowly, but his eyes had clouded. "He is well, he is well enough. I have letters from him—"

He patted his pocket and I looked at the bulge there with hungry eyes.

"But there *is* something he will not have said in the letters."

He looked at Father, who nodded with kind eyes. "Yes, Magnus."

"Well, Brother Jonsson, the Lutheran minister—"

Mr. Stefansson! I should have guessed.

"He places much of the blame on the head of your father. He had to have someone to blame—" He shrugged his shoulders. "I'm sure your going hurt more than some of the others. He went to your house the week you left and he told your father that you had shamed him beyond forgiveness, that both together, son and father, had shamed the church, so Arni Jonsson was no longer welcome to worship there—"

I heard my mother gasp. I clenched my fingers. My father lowered his eyes. "They've been friends since childhood. Sveinn Stefansson married my father and mother, buried their parents, buried their dead sons . . ." His voice was almost a whisper. The room had gone silent.

"He has not been back inside the church, then?" It was Petur who asked it.

Elder Thorderson shook his head. Petur stood. I could see anger in his face and the lines of his body.

"It's not fair for him to be punished for what we've done!"

He turned and left the house. No one tried to stop him, not even my quiet mother.

"It is too bad." Elder Thorderson's voice was as low as my father's. "It is not easy to see an innocent loved one suffer."

A soft expression played over my father's face. "Hasn't it always been innocent people who suffer? It puts us, after all, in good company."

He crossed the room and placed his hand on the younger man's shoulder. "To suffer for the sake of Him who suffered for us, Magnus, is an honor. Even when it is unsought and unrecognized."

Somehow that helped—how did it help? I'm not certain. I assisted my mother in cutting bread and setting dishes for dinner. Petur came back inside and, before he knew it, Magnus had him telling proudly about his job here and answering questions concerning Zion.

I looked on and listened with pleasure. And there was among us that Christmas a sense of peace, a sense of being somehow not far from that Savior who, perfect though he was, had suffered for us, and who could, therefore, both understand and sanctify our own sufferings—and love us for them. We felt that love as we had never felt it since leaving Iceland.

We waited to read the letters. I'm glad we did. There was no school, so the following morning after chores were completed we gathered around the table and read out loud the words from Grandfather Jonsson. My father read them, in a voice that sounded so much like his father's that I could close my eyes and picture my grandfather there. It hurt to open them up and see him missing.

There was nothing but love and concern in the letter; no pettiness, no complaint—no mention of Sveinn Stefansson by name. His words had the poetry and flow of Iceland in them:

I hold you warm in my heart. Like the cry of the ocean—water and wind and sea bird together. I hold your voices and your eyes and the sound of your laughter. When I am lonely I take out my memories, and you are with me. When I am downhearted I sing the old lullabies to you, and know that your sore hearts can hear my song. Be brave, my children. Remember your father. Be happy—keep Iceland alive in your hearts. Then we will never really be separated.

I wiped the tears from my stinging eyes. My father's fingers trembled as he refolded the pages.

"He will die soon," my mother said.

"Yes, Margret. I know he will die. He is dying already."

"And will he not be buried in holy ground, nor his praises sung in the church for the people's remembrance?" Petur's voice was so heavy with pain that I turned my eyes from him. But Father held Petur's gaze with his own.

"His friends will remember. Those who love Arni Jonsson will honor him in their hearts. And he will be buried in Icelandic soil— any corner in Iceland will be hallowed ground if they lay him there."

I went outside and up past the house to read my own letter. I was afraid to read the words. My friendship with Halldor was one of the treasures I had brought with me from Iceland, a relic wrapped in old memory for safekeeping, not something to be taken out overmuch and gazed at, lest the brightness tarnish, the colors dull. This paper I held in my hands had the power to break the relic to bits, to destroy it altogether.

I looked off to the far white mountains. How tranquil they seemed—so removed from my petty pain, from fear or foreboding. I read one by one the words which my friend had written:

Dear Anna: The days in Iceland are fine now. Men prepare for the early fishing and the women reapportion the precious stores with an eye out for spring. I sit on the rock where we played together and look off beyond the ocean and think of you.

My father says you are bad, Anna. But I don't believe his words, for I know your heart. He says I must not write letters to you or even mention your name. But I write to you, Anna —every day some little word or two in my heart, to fly where the far gulls fly, where my feet can't follow. And this time I wrote the words down, Anna, and gave them to your friend, Magnus Thorderson. You may not read any more of my words for a long time. So I will tell you for once and for all, I love you, Anna. You are the best friend I ever have had, and I will not forget you. And no matter how many say it, I will not believe that you have done anything dark or dishonest or evil.

I wish we had said goodbye—but then, could we have done it? Perhaps it is better this way. How much I shall miss you. Miss me, too, Anna! I know you do! Don't forget me. We shall be friends until we are old women—we shall tell our children about each other, and I shall say to my own daughters, "I hope someday you will have a friend, just one friend like my Anna."

Tears blurred the words till I could not read them. I hugged the letter to me. It was a fire inside, a fire with power to burn, but also to light me. I knew it would be that way for a long, long time.

Chapter Nine

I went back to school, but Samuel did not go with me. He had contracted a fever and complained of pains in his throat. I was worried about him. Mother checked for signs of diphtheria and found them: deposits on his tonsils, swollen glands. Sometimes what appear to be only mild cases are really the worst ones. He grew weaker and the membranes swelled and the cough developed. Mother started the medication: aconite given alternately with belladonna and a cup of hot beef tea every few hours.

After a few days, as he improved some, I took his meal trays to him, even brought work home for him from school which he struggled to do. Such a gentle sufferer, Samuel. But I was distracted. Two things consumed my vain attention: Elder Thorderson and the spelling bee.

I saw less than I liked of my dear, handsome missionary, even though I contrived ways to bump into him—accidental meetings here and there. How they stirred my senses and gave meaning to the clothes I wore and the wave of my hair and the way my lips curved in a smile! Sunday meetings took on a new importance now, since he would be there. I don't know if my mother noticed how prompt I was, how groomed my appearance, and how cheerfully I helped with the little ones, all with one purpose in mind: to impress him.

Father surely suspected the truth, for one Sunday after meeting he put his hand gently on my shoulder and spoke into my ear: "We are here to adore God, my Anna, not man." He said it gently, but still I blushed. Did it show that plainly? Only to Father, I hoped, who knew me so well. I would be more demure, I resolved. But the very next Sunday I sat beside Elder Thorderson in meeting and he turned when the meeting had ended and said with a smile, "I could not help noticing what a lovely voice you have, Anna. You must sing more. A voice like yours should not be wasted."

I basked in his praise. And I sang. I sang while cooking, while scrubbing the clothes with lye soap, while drying the dishes, while walking back and forth to school—and each song I sang was a tender offering to him who had praised me.

I also spoke out loud while I walked home from school, repeating the words on the spelling list over and over. I had moved to the ranks of the top students. There were some who did better than I in some subjects—most did better, of course, with the English. But none—not one could memorize words as I could. Well, of course two or three might prove some competition to me when it came down to an actual contest. I might be nervous. I might forget, might make a mistake. It could happen. But in my heart I knew I could win—I could win!

Petur encouraged me. He was on top of the world now. He had made friends with some of the older boys who, as young men will do, respected Petur for the brave stand he had taken against the Welsh boys. He was a hero of sorts in their eyes, and he knew it. He earned money. That made him feel like a man. If at times the pendulum swung and despair would grip him as he grappled with some injustice of life, by and large he was right where he wanted to be, and quite smug about it. But that was Petur's way.

I said nothing to Father. I almost felt it would be bad luck. If I happened to win, let it come as a surprise to both Father and Mother. That would sweeten the victory for them.

Samuel watched me. "I'm going to be there," he promised between coughs.

"Then you'd better eat every last bite on this plate," I responded. "And lick the last drop of medicine Mother gives you." He made a face, but he didn't protest. If this could help him—if anything could help him!

The day came at last. At last and too soon. I was surely ready —I had been ready, I knew, for weeks. Then why this weakness in my muscles? This hard knot inside?

The contest was to be held at the schoolhouse in the evening, following chores. I was in a panic getting the young ones dressed and combed. And as for Samuel, I knew his heart was set on going, but Mother said no. She was the nurse, the one who knew such things. I found her alone and begged her permission. She softened a little. "I'll see what your father says." She would go that far. I helped Samuel bathe from the basin and brushed his hair back and buttoned his good shirt on under his nightshirt, just in case.

Father was late coming home that night. We kept supper for him. That only added to my sense of confusion and dread. Mother told him how I had pestered her for permission. He teased me a little.

"Is my Anna competing tonight? She said nothing to me. I had meant to mend that old harness this evening."

My heart leapt into my throat. I felt foolish. I wanted to win, for him, a thousand times more than I ever had.

"I'll go talk to the boy," he said. He went back to Samuel. After long minutes beside his bed he came back to the kitchen.

"I think if we wrap the boy warmly, Margret."

"Suit yourself," my mother said, and her tone was empty.

"Something to look forward to—it has helped him already. Might do more harm to make him stay home—"

"Suit yourself. That's why I asked you, Einar." She turned to fetch the little ones' wraps. She was like that. Not one who likes to give in. She had asked him—but he hadn't made the decision she felt was right. I thought she gave me a little hard look in passing. But I decided not to mind it. The night was mine. And Samuel would be there!

The schoolhouse was crowded to overflowing. The windows were steamed with the heat of the stoked stove and so many bodies. Babies cried and little boys tumbled and darted and poked at each other through parents' legs. I took my seat on the stand with the line of contestants. My throat felt sore and tight when I swallowed. So many people! A sea of faces. They seemed to be friendly. They were looking forward to more than this spelling bee. There was a pie-baking contest and the entries would serve as refreshments. There would be games for the little children. I swallowed again. My teacher stood and the room became gradually quiet. There was an opening prayer and a song, but I scarcely heard them. I was searching out *my* faces, the ones I had chosen, the ones I would spell to tonight.

The others were standing. I stood and licked my dry lips and straightened my skirt. We stepped forward. We took our appointed places. There were ten of us in the line. The faces went watchful. Some of them no longer looked so friendly. Miss Fletcher gave the first word. Maria spelled it in her voice that was soft as a swirl of icing. I kept my eyes on Samuel's face and waited my turn.

Pendulum . . . interruption . . . consideration . . . spontaneous . . . susceptible . . . one by one I spelled the words that were mine. As I spelled them I counted them off, like a game: This one is for Samuel—the first for Samuel. Father next. Then Mother—that one made her sit up a little. With each word I seemed to relax. Now for Petur, who thinks he is the only smart Icelander here. *Philistine* for Elder Thorderson—he'll like that. Then back again to Samuel.

The line grew shorter. The line shrank until there were just two standing: myself and Miriam, the girl with the yellow braid who had laughed and whispered and pointed at me my first day in school. I would show her. I found my faces: Father, Samuel, Elder —there, right there leaning on his elbow and looking cocky, blocking my view of Elder Thorderson—there he was, the Welsh boy!

I met his eyes; I couldn't help it. The blue in the round eyes sparkled. Then very quickly one of the blue eyes closed in a wink. Had I really seen it? I turned my eyes away, but my cheeks were burning. My voice sounded strange, I thought, as I spelled the next word.

With an effort I pulled back my concentration. The words grew more difficult. I forgot the audience, my faces, even the Welsh boy, and lived only for each word as I heard it pronounced.

Then it happened. All of a sudden, with no warning, no fanfare. Miss Fletcher said, "Miriam, would you please spell the word *paraphernalia* for us." A blank look crossed Miriam's features. She tried it. But it was guesswork from the beginning. Miss Fletcher turned toward me.

The whole room seemed to turn toward me and hold its breath. I spelled *paraphernalia* without a flaw: p-a-r-a-p-h-e-r-n-a-l-i-a. Miss Fletcher smiled. I heard a voice from somewhere in the back shout, "Bully for Anna!" I searched for my father's eyes but I saw the Welsh boy, his mouth wide open in a grin.

I was smiling. I couldn't help myself. Miss Fletcher took a few steps and walked to the table. Miriam sniffled. "So, she can spell the words," she sneered in a very loud whisper. "She can't tell you what one of them means!"

The room seemed to go quiet. A few boys standing near the table snickered. "Go on, ask Anna what the words mean!" one of them shouted. There was laughter now. Miriam turned to me.

"Definition of *paraphernalia*," she began very primly. "Collection of articles, apparatus, trappings or gear." She pulled her mouth into a tight little line. "There, Anna, I did that one for you. Why don't you define *ominous* for us. Go on."

She stood there waiting. The whole room leaned forward, waiting. I tried to breathe. I tried to frame sounds in my throat. But the sounds stuck there. The terrible truth was: I could not define the word. Not *ominous*, not *paraphernalia*, not *spontaneous* — not even *Philistine*. She was right — she was cruelly right!

Miss Fletcher stepped forward. She had a book in her hands and a paper. Where she gripped them the knuckles on her hand had gone white.

"We shall attempt to ignore Miriam's rude behavior," she said in careful, clipped tones, her eyes on the water spot in the ceiling above us. "This is a spelling competition; nothing more, nothing less. Anna won it fairly. Anna Jonsson is by far the best speller I have in my school."

There was a smatter of scattered applause, much like the sound spring rain makes, I thought, running over glass. She held the book out to me. "Your prize, Miss Jonsson, with our warmest congratulations." She clapped her hands. A small, feminine gesture. Still clapping, she turned to face the audience. Not until then did a few hands really start clapping with hers, then more and more, until the room was filled with the sound.

The sound meant nothing to me, nor the friendly faces, nor the people who pushed forward to congratulate me. I felt no pride, no joy, only burning shame. She was right! I was only a trained parrot, empty-headed, good for nothing. I felt exposed. I wanted desperately to hide! Where were my faces? They mustn't find me. How could I meet their eyes?

I pushed my way toward the door with my eyes averted. *Please let me make it! Let me disappear,* I prayed.

I stepped outside. The darkness had never been kinder. With the cold night air it numbed my senses, it obliterated my wretched identity. I took a deep breath and shivered. I heard nothing. But there was a hand on my arm that slid down till it found my cold fingers.

"Let's walk, Anna."

I didn't protest, but stumbled a little way, led by his hand. "You can't comfort me this time, Father, so don't even bother."

"It's no bother," he laughed. "It's a madhouse in there. And it's not comfort I've come to give you, but strength." He put his arm around my shoulder. His warmth made me shake.

"You were magnificent up there, Anna."

I drew away. "I made a fool of myself."

He answered me sharply. "You threaten to make a fool of yourself right now." His voice was a growl. "But up there you were magnificent—clear to the end."

I shook my head. The tears were pushing. "You don't understand!" My voice had a tremble in it. "She was right! She was right and she knew it. She won in the end."

My father shook his head. "You're so stubborn, Anna. Didn't you listen to your teacher? Don't you know? Didn't you feel the love and pride all around you?"

I shook my head again. His voice was too gentle. It made me go weak.

"For the Holy One of Israel shall execute judgment in righteousnesss," he quoted, his voice warm and firm. "And the righteous need not fear, for they are those who shall not be confounded."

"That doesn't sound like Icelandic poetry," I complained.

"It's from there." He tapped the book I held. I looked down at the cover. Book of Mormon. I let my father guide me back under the halo of light near the building's entrance. Here I opened the book. It was signed inside. Signed to me by my lovely teacher. But how had she known? How had she known the book would be mine?

"Let's go back inside, daughter, before anyone catches us gone." Before we entered he squeezed my hand and whispered, "You'll be all right. I've no doubt of that, Anna."

He was right. I held up my head and smiled at the people who were kind enough to congratulate me. I talked and I laughed and the pain subsided. And when Elder Thorderson brought me a piece of my favorite pie I saw no pity in his eyes.

When the evening was over Petur carried Samuel out to the wagon. His eyes were bright, too bright. I held his hand. It was like a small coal against mine. "Oh, Samuel," I said as I kissed his forehead. "It meant so much more to win knowing you were there."

"You won for both of us, Anna, for all the Icelanders." I nodded. His voice seemed as light as air. "Don't let that awful girl matter, Anna. You won't let her matter?"

I bent low and whispered against his ear. "No, Samuel. As long as you're proud of me, nothing else matters at all."

I held his hand the entire way home. When we got inside Mother chased everyone else away and cared for him herself. There was a look behind her eyes that frightened me badly. Had we made the wrong decision in letting him go? I thought of asking Father, but something stopped me. Perhaps fear of what his reply might be.

I placed my certificate with the gold seal and my new Book of Mormon on the shawl with my other books and treasures.

"You earned that doubly, Anna." The voice was Petur's. I looked up and smiled, but he scowled in return. "That wouldn't

have happened to you if you came from Scotland, or *Wales*"—he
spat out the word—"or even Norway. But because you are Icelandic—"

"It's all right, Petur."

"Did Father convince you of that?" His eyes were live fires.
"His saying so doesn't make it that way." He struck his fist against
the bed where the force was soundless. The quilt crumpled and
the mattress quivered like jelly. "You didn't see Samuel's face. I
did." He clenched his fist again. "Tell me that's all right, Anna.
Well, go ahead."

There was nothing I could say. I turned back to my treasures.
Petur would have things either black or white, never shades
between. Hot or cold. Pain or ecstasy. That was Petur.

I picked up my new Book of Mormon. I had thought it would
be a good idea to read in the book every night before going to
sleep. I didn't feel much like it now, but that made no difference. I
was determined to keep the resolve I had made.

Chapter Ten

I didn't go to school the following morning. Samuel became quite
sick during the night and Mother asked if I might stay home to
help her. She must have been terribly worried herself to make
such a request. In the main I was relieved at not going. But I
couldn't resist a thought or two about what I was missing. Would
the praise have outweighed the teasing and ridicule? Would Miss
Fletcher be disappointed? Would the Welsh boy miss me?

By mid-morning all thoughts of myself had fled. Samuel was
in a bad way and I knew it. I did the cooking and cleaning and
hovered on the edges of the line my mother had drawn marking
her domain—the corner that was her sickroom, her sanctuary,
where she fought against pain and death for the life of her son.

That night over dinner Father was silent and thoughtful. "They will be letting some of the men go," he said under his breath. "Just for the next few months till the weather breaks and the ground dries. There is not work enough right now." He glanced over at Petur. "I think we had better be ready—"

But Petur dismissed him. "Nonsense, Father, there's no way they'll fire us. We're the hardest workers they have, and they know it!" He went on to boast and tease, but my father's features retained the imprint of his own fears.

Samuel didn't get better. The foul-smelling deposits spread through the passages into his nose and ears. He would toss and turn with a terrible moaning, then fall into a stupor that seemed like death. Mother would take his hard, small pulse and sit beside him. Every hour she forced down the belladonna and another medication the doctor had brought that smelled strongly of iodine. We watched and waited.

The next afternoon Petur came home early. I felt nothing at first but relief at seeing him there. He could lift the heavy washtub for me and help Gesli haul up the big pieces of wood. The day had turned cold and a storm was threatening, and the house must be as warm for Samuel as we could make it.

In my preoccupation with Samuel I noticed nothing. Unthinking, I laid out the chores I wanted done. Petur stared at me; he stared straight through me. He made no move, no sign he had even heard. I heard Samuel in a fit of coughing; Mother called me. I turned away from the empty eyes and went back to her.

Not until the meal was on the table and Father seated and the hot potatoes cooled in their jackets did Petur return. He had washed face and hands outside at the pump. He sat down in silence and began eating in hungry gulps. I watched him. And suddenly I knew. I put down my fork and, without thinking, chose from my compassion words that were hard and cruel.

"They let you go! That's what happened, isn't it, Petur? Earlier when you came home I didn't . . ."

I stopped. My father had held up his hand. My mother stopped eating. Even Gesli and little Sina sat still.

"They let me go, all right. There were five hired after—five all younger than *me*, and they let me go!"

"There'll be more tomorrow." My father's quiet words were like blows to Petur.

"More tomorrow—and the first to go an Icelander! They found no fault with me or my work—Brother Pearson said so. Then why else was it *me* they let go? *Why, Father?*"

Petur was shouting the words. Father rose from the table. "There is a sick child in this house. You will lower your voice, son."

"You will speak more respectfully to your father." It was my mother, and her voice held a hidden menace.

Petur looked from one to the other, then pushed back his chair, or rather the side of the bench where he sat so that Gesli teetered and his fork clattered down to the floor. Petur stood. His eyes were like stones, but his body trembled.

"There's a freight wagon in the canyon this side of Provo." He said the words slowly—ordinary words, but by the way he spoke them I knew he had rehearsed them to himself many times before.

"They're moving out tomorrow morning and I can go with them. They've offered me a position—one of their men broke his leg in a bust-up down Emigration."

Petur stopped. He had reached the first stage. He looked at my father. My father made a mistake. He sat down to the table.

"Sit down and finish your food, Petur."

My father began to eat as though nothing had happened. Petur stared at the top of his head for a moment.

"What gear can I take that is mine, that you might spare?"

My father didn't look up, but his voice was louder, with a note in it Petur would have done well to heed—if he had not been past heeding.

"Petur, I will not hear such talk. You insult me, you—"

"No, Father, you insult me by making me crawl off like a whipped cur to lick my wounds, by expecting me—"

"I expect nothing, save what you ought to expect from yourself." My father spoke quietly. This time his words were like feathers, floating and disembodied from brain or flesh. "Dignity and self-respect, Petur."

"Words, Father!" Petur pushed back his hair. "Other men assign or deny dignity, Father, and determine how much a man can respect himself."

My father shook his head. He looked up at Petur. "I will tell you one more time, son, sit down to your meal. To talk as you have been talking is wicked."

Petur pushed his hair back from his forehead again with a hand that was more a fist. "I am going, Father."

"Not now, Petur!" I spoke without meaning to. "Samuel is so sick. We need you. You can't just walk away."

"And where would you go?" It was my mother, my practical mother. I think she expected to uncover his shallow resolves that were empty of plan. He surprised us all by calmly replying, "I'll go to the end of the line with the drovers, then take passage on ship to New Orleans. From there—"

He paused and cocked his head a little and shifted his eyes so they met none of ours.

"From there I think I'll take passage back home."

There was silence; no response, no sound of breath drawn, no movement. Even the little ones sat frozen still.

"I don't belong here. I've learned that much since—"

"You have learned nothing. Nothing! Do you know what it is you say—what it is you reject? Do not make me ashamed of you, Petur."

Petur's face went pale. His eyes were dark hollows masking pain I could not imagine.

"I'm sorry, Father. I've made up my mind; I'm going home. Grandfather could use my help—we have holdings to work there."

"I thought this was home." Gesli said it softly; small words, but brittle as pebbles thrown over ice.

"This is home now, Gesli," my father responded. "Petur will not find what he is looking for back in Iceland."

Petur shrugged his shoulders, a little-boy gesture. The pain threatened to spill into sight.

"I'm no use to you here—a burden, not earning my way . . ." He shuffled a few steps backward.

My father stared at him. "What you are saying is nonsense— weak arguments to support a weakness you've harbored inside. Walk through that door if you feel you must, Petur. I believe you will be making a foolish mistake if you do."

It was the moment that pushed the resolve. Petur acted. There was no last look, no word of farewell. He turned from us, walked through the door, and drew it closed behind him. I started to rise.

"Sit down and finish your supper, daughter."

I sat still for my father's sake, but I could not swallow, could not bear the sight of the food. This silence was like a hand pressed against my throat.

He'll be back! my heart said. Perhaps all of us clung to that thought in the naked silence. *He'll spend the night with one of his friends—or with Elder Thorderson.* That would be good. No one would be better than Elder Thorderson to soften his mind.

I watched beside Samuel. It was a bad night for Samuel. Sitting there in the darkness I prayed—one prayer only that pushed its way past all others: *Don't let this happen to my mother, dear Lord. Don't let her lose two sons after losing her baby daughter.*

By dawn there was still no sign of change in Samuel. I rose and went to the window. The sky was pale—pale and gray and empty. No rosiness to it, so softness, no promise of day.

Not till later that morning when Gesli came in from his outside chores did I learn how resolved, how thorough my Petur had been. He had taken his clothes and belongings outside to the barn—the lean-to barn that was shared by several families who housed their animals there. It had housed for a moment the anger and pain and dreams of a frightened young man.

The sun did rise, the full day did come upon us. There was breath to draw and work to do, and living that must go on. I knew that. But I wondered how other hearts handled the pain. Did they hurt as much inside as I did? I watched my mother's face; there was no way of telling. But when my father came home from work I avoided his eyes. I could not stand to see my own anguish reflected in them, nor the hopelessness, nor the questioning why.

Chapter Eleven

That night the crisis came. My father called Elder Thorderson in and together they placed hands upon Samuel's head and appealed to that Father who had given them license to act in his name, to invoke his power, to turn to him in their need. I felt some of the sweetness pour through me, just standing there listening, closing my eyes. Petur's name was not mentioned, nor his absence noted. But less than an hour after that blessing was given the fever broke, the sensation of suffocation lifted, and we knew that Samuel would live.

Much later, after reading my Book of Mormon, I prayed. I thought someone ought to say thank you. Some people claim there is no God, and others that the power that rules the universe is not a being, but an immense and mystical force with no soul, no feelings, no connection that can be traced to man. I know other-wise. I believe this Father loves us the way my own father does. He had reached down to bless us today. Perhaps in the future he would find it within his heart and his purposes to bless us again.

I believe I had almost forgotten that school existed. Too much had happened to swallow my days and consume my thoughts. It was now March, which is really spring, though it didn't feel it. I walked to the pump. Though Samuel had turned for the better, he still needed careful care. My mother was with him. There were dozens of things for me to do in her stead.

I didn't hear the sound of steps coming from behind me. The moist earth muffled the cautious feet. I looked up to see him standing there, staring. I wondered how long he had been watch-ing me.

Owen grinned and held out his hand. "I brought these for you. How's your brother?"

I took the pussy willows and rubbed their softness against my cheek. "Samuel's fever broke last night. This was—these are—

thank you. I like pussy willows." I shifted the branches so that for a moment they blotted my face from his view.

His blue eyes danced. "I knew you'd like them. Now that your brother's getting well, will you come back to school?"

"Oh yes, I suppose—as soon as my mother lets me." Why was I having such trouble talking to him? He seemed natural and at his ease, as though what was happening was an everyday occurrence. I wondered if he had ever been up on the Iceland bench before.

"Have I missed very much?" I asked. "While I've been absent?"

"Nothing you couldn't make up like that!" He snapped his fingers and his grin covered his whole face. "Really, Anna, it's been as boring as Sunday meeting without you there."

I had never before heard him speak my name, not directly to me. I had never called him by his. Owen Davies. Why had he come up here to see me?

"How's your brother, Petur?"

"How's Petur?" The question stung me. My mind struggled to form a reply. "Why are you asking?"

"No reason." He looked hard at the ground a minute. "Well, actually, Anna, I saw what happened."

What happened! I swallowed a sense of panic, a dryness that tightened my throat.

"She's really not a very nice girl, Molly. He asked her there— right there on the street, and she turned him down."

I was burning with curiosity. "What did he ask her?"

Owen looked closely at me. "Didn't he tell you? He just asked her to go to the dance with him—and he thinks she turned him down because he's Icelandic. But that wasn't it—" His blue eyes narrowed into a squint-line of concentration. I had seen it before. "She turned him down because that's her way—she's like that. She likes to make people squirm."

His directness, rather than embarrassing me or frightening me, seemed a strange comfort, a relief of sorts.

"Aw, don't worry about it, Anna. Don't look so solemn."

I smiled and the furrowed squint disappeared.

"I just thought perhaps you might say something—you know, so Petur won't take it so personal-like."

I nodded. *I'd love to say something—I'd love to say something!* I would love to have called Petur back. I could see him, marching out to test his conclusions, fresh from dismissal—throwing himself on the mercy of Molly Brown. Just another boy put in his place by Molly. But this time it had been more than that.

"Thanks for coming, Owen. I'd better be going. Mother's waiting—" I glanced at the water pail.

"I'll carry that for you." He took it from me. It was only a little way, but I couldn't protest. Before the words came for me to say we had reached my door.

He set the bucket down and I tried to thank him. But he shook his head and his brown curls bounced.

"I'll see you, Anna Jonsson, I'll see you."

He turned and raced down the hill. He bounded, like a small deer or a mountain pony on his short, sure legs.

What had he meant when he said, "I'll see you"? I was sure it was something more than just meeting at school.

Samuel was young. Once the crisis was over he grew noticeably stronger every day. My mother adjusted his medication and administered it less frequently, making sure he consumed his broth and the teas we brought him. She could still fill her mind and her hours with him.

For my father it was another thing altogether. He went daily out into the world which his son had rejected. He met the faces and the questions, and sometimes the silence that was more cruel than the cruelest of jests and accusations. It was hard to grasp the reality: Petur was gone. In all this broad, wide world, where was he? Was he safe or was he suffering? What was he thinking? Would he really go all the way back to Iceland? And the question that tore at my heart with familiar fingers: Would I ever in this life see Petur again?

Hadn't this happened once before in a world of strangers, when a baby was snatched from her mother's arms? Not taken cleanly by death, not safe and buried, but suspended in a nightmare that never could cease. It was much the same with Petur; we had no way of knowing, nothing beyond uncertainty. True, he was not a baby, not a child, but a man nearly grown; he had turned nineteen years old on his last birthday. This was easier for my mother than Dena had been; not so with my father. It is hard to say how it was with him.

He felt most of all the shame of what Petur was doing. As an Icelander he believed that God's eyes were upon us. What we did for ill or good would be seen by the heavens and last as long as the earth lasted, and live on in the world of men after we were gone. Petur had shamed himself, his father, his ancestors, and his unborn sons—not to speak of the God whom his action dishonored. The shame would live in my father's heart beyond even the pain.

A week later I went back to school. It was good to have something to sink my teeth into, to drown myself in. Miss Fletcher was kind, and Owen Davies did his best to turn my world upside down. At lunchtime he brought his black bucket to where I sat and sat down beside me. At first we said very little, but ate in silence. I was aware of the sound my teeth made chewing, and when I swallowed it seemed the food stuck in my throat.

He offered me a piece of fresh bread spread with butter and a thick slab of cheese he had placed on top. I took it with hesitation; I had little to offer. I didn't like taking favors from anyone. But he seemed so pleased at the giving that I couldn't resist it. We said small things to one another. I tried to avoid any subject that might draw us close to Petur. His directness presented a danger. Of course I knew that some time or other the truth would come out, but not this way. I didn't want to discuss the matter with him; I didn't want to answer his wide-eyed questions.

One day, then two, then three we ate lunch together. I was beginning at last to relax a little. Spring helped in that process. The days were lovely, the air warm and dry and filled with birdsong. I thought of the puffins and the white graceful seagulls. I said to Owen, "Have you ever wished that you lived by the sea?"

"I lived by the sea in Wales," he answered.

I checked an urge to reach out and touch him. "Close by it? Close enough to hear and smell it?"

He shook his head. "Not that close. But at times I would run away there. Take a lunch and fish in the estuary shallows."

"Do you miss the sea?" I asked him.

"At times I miss it. Now and again." He looked at me carefully, eyes wide open. "You miss it all the time, don't you?"

I nodded my head.

"There's nothing I miss that much."

I stared at him. I wanted to say, *I miss everything that much, Owen. Everything that was home.*

That evening I took my book of Icelandic poetry from its shelf and climbed to a little point I had discovered above the bench line, a smooth strip of grass with a slim outcropping of hollowed rock where I would often sit and read or write or gaze off to the distance, the line of mountain and sky that was always changing, alive to the shadows of evening, the colors of dawn, the play of cloud and weather across it.

I closed my eyes. I could see as plain as those mountains the stretch of shoreline where my grandfather had stood as he waved goodbye, with the mewing of gulls in the air and the cliffs above him, and our house nestled down in the hollow just over the rise. Gone, all gone. Would my grandfather stand there and watch the sea bring his grandson back to him? Would they embrace with the tide curling around their ankles?

I found a verse that was one of my favorites. I read it over, then closed my eyes and said it inside my head. I had known the words by heart since I could remember:

> The sun is on yon heights! and from these cliffs
> It speaks to us of love and glory there,
> Like some fresh joyous angel that alights
> To call us upward to the good and fair.
>
> It says the better Sun is just at hand,
> And with Him all true dayspring. O Great Sun,
> Sun of all earth and heaven, ascend and shine,
> And let this darkness pass, this night be done.

It was spring; the sun on the heights warmed me. But would night ever loosen its dark hold on us as long as Petur remained a mystery and a shame? I stretched. The shadows of evening crept down from the hillside and covered my head, shadows of rose and lavender, cool, welcome shadows. I felt as cool and soft as the shadows. Was I disloyal to feel happiness seep from the shadows down into me, and to welcome the happiness, hold out my two hands for it, eager and wanting and self-contained?

Owen knew. All the next day at school he seemed different, and several times during the day I caught his eyes on me, not wide and open, but crinkled and troubled.

I avoided him at lunch. There was one way to do that: stay in and help Miss Fletcher. Perhaps she knew, or at least sensed some need on my part. I knew Owen would never approach the subject in her presence.

When school was over I slipped out of my seat and into the schoolyard, walking as fast as I dared without drawing attention. I was nearly a block away when he caught up with me. He came softly from behind and matched his stride to my own. I slowed down some. It was fruitless now to try to avoid him. I drew in my breath. I might as well get it done and over.

"Listen, Anna," he said, "don't be angry with me. What have I done to upset you?"

"Nothing yet. But you will. So just go ahead, Owen, ask your questions."

"I don't have any questions to ask," he replied, and his voice had grown wary. "You're so obstinate, Anna. I meant nothing. I only wanted to tell you I understand."

He stopped a moment. I think I was glaring at him, daring him to be kind. "You understand, do you. Just what do you understand?"

He made one more attempt. "Don't be angry, Anna. No one blames Petur for going away."

"That's not true. The Icelandic men all do. And the brethren who are not Icelandic shake their heads and whisper behind their hands: Here's one convert who wasn't of strong enough stock—a weakling who left the kingdom for the ways of the world. A disgrace."

Owen's eyes grew wide. "That's nonsense, Anna. There may be one or two who say that, but they don't count. You can't worry over that kind."

"*You* can say that. It wasn't your brother who ran away. It isn't your father who has to walk with his head bowed in shame."

"It can't be as bad as you make it sound." Owen picked a stone up and skipped it along the edge of the road where it bounced and skittered. "Why do you always make things seem worse than they really are, Anna?"

It made me angry to hear him say that. "For all you know, things are worse than I make them seem."

He laughed then. But I refused to budge an inch. I'm not certain why. We had reached the end of the path that led up to our dugout and the homes of the other Icelanders. I stopped in my tracks.

"You'd better go back," I said. He cocked his head at me. "You'd better not be seen on the hill with an Icelandic girl."

I turned and began to walk. He stood, waiting. "Don't you want me to walk with you, Anna?"

Of course I do! But how can I say so out loud? I was angry. He had placed the whole thing onto my shoulders. It wasn't fair.

"No, I want you to leave me alone, Owen."

I said the words over my shoulder. I didn't turn, didn't pause to see what he would do. He stood there a moment. "Suit yourself," he said very softly. "I'll see you, Anna."

I didn't turn. I didn't reply. My eyes were stinging with weak, girlish tears. How I hated myself as I hurried up the hill! By the time I finally turned and looked behind there was no sign of Owen. The path was bare. Bare and lonely and silent. I walked on alone.

Chapter Twelve

Spring was upon us. There was ground to prepare and new seed to be sown. My father had chosen a site for our house and had dug a foundation, bit by bit through the past two months, in what spare time he had. He was purchasing the land from another Icelander, paying partly in kind, with the work of his hands. He was doing the fine inside woodwork for Brother Sturleson as well as making a long sturdy table with chairs to match.

The work for my father to do—it was never-ending. I knew he missed Petur's strong, capable hands. He rose earlier in the mornings and worked till past sunset and the flesh on his frame grew lean and his thin face gaunt. I wondered if my mother worried about him. She worked silently by his side as always. I never heard her complain or say what she was thinking or feeling. I felt a stranger to both of them.

That Sunday evening following my episode with Owen we went to meeting. For the first time my mother let Samuel go with us. There we sat in the row together—a family again. Yet I was so painfully aware that one of us was missing. His absence seemed something palpable that the other people could turn and see.

At the end of the meeting Brother Palsson made an announcement. A choir, an Icelandic choir, was being organized. There had been talk of doing so for many months now. We were all thrilled to see it come into reality.

On the way home from church Gesli tugged at my silent father. At first he got no response but, being young, he persisted.

"Father," he asked, his face anxious and solemn, "Petur loves to sing most of all of us. Do you think if we wrote him a letter and told him, that he might come home to sing in the choir?"

I sought my mother's eyes, but she turned her face. My father made not a sound. I took Gesli's hand and walked ahead with him and little Sina, trying to explain to his childish mind how someone he loved could disappear—how a tender father could turn cold at the name of his own son.

Later that night I approached my father. I had felt shut off from him for so long. Yet I felt unsure, almost shy at the prospect of chipping a way through his guard. He was reading; something he seldom did anymore. Even now, though the hour was early, he nodded. He would be up long before the sun was up in the morning.

I noticed that the book in his lap was Icelandic. I was somehow glad of that. I sat down by his side, pulling Mother's rocker close. I read what I could of the poems over his shoulder. He stayed on one page, as though staring at the words, not really reading. I hazarded my question. It was not just to draw him. It was something I desperately wanted to know.

"Father, if Petur should write us a letter with an address where we could reach him . . . will you write back?"

I strained forward to sense his mood. His face was averted. He spoke softly. "I don't think he'll write, Anna."

"If he did—if he does—" I felt myself tremble.

"We shall wait and see if he does. This is a subject I don't wish to discuss, not with you, Anna."

I felt the withdrawal in his voice. "But, Father, you've always discussed things with me—even the hard things." It was a breathless protest. He raised his head slowly.

"I'm sorry to hurt you, my Anna. But not this time."

Not this time! I had never heard those words before. I had never felt from him silence—rejection.

"One thing alone I will say." His voice sounded weary, with an edge of anger I could feel. "I echo the poet, and give you my thoughts in the poet's words."

He took the book he had been reading and handed it to me. With one of his fingers he pointed the place, then he walked from the room. I stared at the page a moment, then forced it to focus. The words were the words of Bjarni Thorarenson, one of my favorites:

> The skerry away in the fjord,
> So deep in the sea's unrest,
> In silence endures forever
> The foam that beats on its breast . . .

I could feel the words in my head, and I knew how they ended.

> Mean is the man who is weaker
> Than senseless rock in the strife,
> And yields to the clash of the billows,
> The countering currents of life.

My father, my strong good father, had never yielded. There was nothing inside him to understand the weakness, the giving in of another—especially that of his firstborn son. Perhaps in his heart of hearts he loved still. But I knew now that from out of his strength he had not yet found a way to forgive.

There were just a few weeks left of school. In fact, with the spring sowing, many of the older boys had already dropped out. I went back to school the following Monday half expecting not to see Owen there. Why did the sight of his round, open face send a happiness through me? I was shy of him. How should I act after what I had done? He had probably had his fill of me. Those days when he had contrived for us to eat lunch together, I had not been unaware of the price he paid. His group of Welsh friends dogged him and teased him rudely. And though he had seemed unaffected, I wondered now. Surely I had made it clear that I wasn't worth any such price.

All through the morning I thought my surmise was the right one. Then at lunchtime he sprang from his seat at the very first moment and pushed his way toward me. At that same moment Miss Fletcher looked up from her desk.

"Oh, Anna, would you mind staying in to help me today?"

I stood still, my mouth wide open, my heart beating wildly. Suddenly Owen was at my elbow, his face a wide grin.

"If it's not a matter of life and death, Miss Fletcher, it's important that I eat lunch with Anna today."

A flicker of a smile teased the corners of her mouth. "By all means, Owen. What I have to do can wait. Go ahead, Anna."

He took my hand—*he took my hand*—he had never done that, and led me clear out to the cottonwood tree by the edge of the school grounds. Here the noise of the children was muted. We sat together in a small patch of shade. I could hear a lark sing from the meadow beyond the road and close by me the sound of a bee in the tall grass.

"This may be my last day of school."

That was Owen; he was always one to come right to the point. I nodded. I wanted to say, "I'll miss you." Instead, I asked, "Does your father need your help?"

"Well, he won't admit it. If he had his way I'd stay in school for the next ten years. Go up to Salt Lake and study."

"I'd like to do something like that." Imagine going back to the city I loved and attending school there. It would be like a dream come true.

Owen was grinning. "I guess you would like that. Your eyes are all sparkling, Anna."

I turned my head a little. "That's all right, Anna. I wish I liked school the way you do. Far as I'm concerned, I don't think I'll miss it."

"Won't you be coming back?"

He shook his head. "I'm eighteen—I'm nearly nineteen. If it wasn't for Father I'd never have stuck it out this long. It's time I got to work. Will you come back next year, Anna?"

"I don't know," I said slowly. The truth was that I hadn't thought about it. What would I do? I would soon be nineteen myself. Nineteen seemed a woman, too old for a one-room schoolhouse. But what else was there for me? Staying home to help my mother? Hiring out? I had never once given thought to my future. There had been more than enough to life taking it day by day.

He was watching me again.

"If you don't come back here"—words stuck in my throat when his eyes were on me—"what kind of work will you do with your father?"

"Farming, mostly. He likes that. He's bought as much land as he can and keep clothes on his back. He can't get used to all the land that a man can own here."

"What do you like?"

The grin disappeared and his eyebrows furrowed. "I'm not sure. I like working the land all right. It's nice being out in the fresh air, not down in the hole."

"The hole?"

"The mines back in Wales. My father worked them. So did my brothers Gareth and James."

"Did you?"

"Almost. I was twelve when we came here. Most boys start in the mines before that. But Dada wouldn't let me."

"He wanted something better for you."

Owen nodded. "I'm a bit of a disappointment, I know. Didn't take to book learning the way he wanted."

"What do you take to? What do you like?" I asked him again. I realized I knew little about him and nothing about his family.

"I like music," he said, "and I like to work with my hands. I'd like—" He paused. "Well, someday I'll tell you."

For some reason I didn't push him.

"It's time to go back." Reluctantly he stood and brushed crumbs from his shirt front. I stood myself, before he could help me up. We were close to one another. He seemed to move closer.

"I'll miss you, Anna." He said the words softly—the words that I couldn't say! I looked into his eyes.

"I can see the sea in your eyes," I told him. "The color of the sea back home."

"I'm glad." He didn't smile—he just looked at me. "I see many things in your eyes, Anna. But they're all too deep to get hold of." He touched my hand.

"Will I see you again?" I asked.

He smiled. "God willing. Would you like that, Anna—to see me?"

Why was he like that? Why did he put me on the spot so? I turned my head.

"Never mind," he said, "never mind." And the way he said it sent small shivers along my spine.

All that afternoon I felt miserable inside. Would I see him after school? Would he talk to me once more? When school was over his friends swarmed together in their usual way. He went along with them. He made no attempt to seek me out. I walked home alone, with the sound of his voice in my head: *Never mind, never mind.*

School was over. I didn't miss it as I had expected. There was too much to keep me busy from day to day. If there was anything I missed, it was Petur. At times I felt empty inside when I thought about him. There was no one to fill that emptiness. But for a time Elder Thorderson came almost daily to help Father construct the foundation of the new home.

The walls were to be made of local adobe, the choice "blue adobes" hauled from the Springville spring. But the foundation was to be stone and the laying of mortar was a skill Elder Thorderson shared with only a few.

I think he enjoyed the work and I know he was mindful of what Petur's loss meant to Father, in more ways than one. Some days while he rested and ate he would ask me to read to him in Icelandic. I loved those times, and felt nothing could match the sympathy moving between us.

In addition to working with Mother I helped make bricks, tramping the clay with bare feet until Brother Richards judged the consistency to be right. Then very quickly the men would pour the clay into wooden molds to be set out to dry. I helped arrange the rows of molds in the drying yard. It was messy work, hard on the back, but I didn't mind it. By pitching in that way we saved money and time. When there were enough dry bricks for our home we could have our allotment, though some of the ones we set would not dry until later and would go into houses built after our own. It was that kind of cycle.

The days passed quickly, with no time for thinking or reading, or even catching one's breath.

May passed into June and June slipped by us and the hot, dry days of July set in. On the first Sunday of July, in meeting, Elder Thorderson stood up before us to say goodbye.

Had the congregation known? I looked over their faces. No one else seemed struck and breathless as I. He had an offer for a good job in Salt Lake City, and he felt he should take it. There were many here it was painful for him to leave, some who were as his own family. His eyes found mine. I knew mine were filled with tears, but that didn't matter. Nothing mattered any more.

That evening he came to our house. This was not unusual. But he asked if I might walk with him. My father consented. We went up above the dugouts. The meadows were dry. I kicked at a clump of sage, green-gray, brittle as a broom.

He seemed sad. But I was too sad to help him. At last he said softly, "My little Anna, I am sorry to cause you pain with my leaving."

Was the pain then only mine? "Won't you miss me?" How petty a thing to ask!

"Of course I shall. More than I want to admit. But, Anna . . . what you think, what you want would not work for us."

What did he mean? What was he saying exactly? I knew, but I did not want to know.

"How I care for you is not exactly the way of a sister. It is more the way of a man for a woman—I think you know that."

My heart soared in ridiculous hope. But his words continued.

"Perhaps it has been wrong of me, Anna, to care for you in that way. You are so young and—"

I wanted to reach for his hand, the way Owen had reached for mine. How old was he? Twenty-seven, twenty-eight? That could hardly matter. I was nearly nineteen. I was nearly a woman.

"There is a girl in Salt Lake City, Anna. I have known her since I was a child. When I go there I shall ask her to be my wife."

I wound my fingers around and around in a knot till they ached.

"Oh, Anna, do not look at me with those eyes. How I hate to hurt you!"

He turned away, and I knew that his pain was real. "It would never work. You are too young, Anna. And I am too old, and—a thousand things."

He turned back to me. "You will be happy, Anna. I know that. You have something within you—"

I shook my head. "I have nothing! Not you, not Petur—" *Not Owen.* I turned from his eyes. He touched me, very gently, on the shoulder.

"Please, Anna. If I loved you less than I do, I would not have told you. But I could not bear to have you find out any other way."

I stood still beneath his hand. What could I tell him? What would make any difference now?

"Will you promise me one thing, Anna?"

"What is it?"

He drew a long breath. I knew this was hard for him. "Will you join the choir, Anna, and sing? I would like that. I would like to think of you using your beautiful voice."

I was silent.

"Will you do it for me?" he added.

I wanted to deny him, but how could I? He who had taught us the gospel, who had sacrificed for us, who had loved and understood, who had given so much?

"Yes," I replied, "I will sing for you." And I meant it. All the music of my heart still belonged to him.

He turned me to face him again. "I will leave you now, Anna. Would you like me to go down first?" I nodded.

Then he took my face in his hands. The touch of his fingers was like trails of molten gold traced along my skin. He kissed me on the cheek. "Goodbye, little Anna. May the Lord bless and keep you."

He turned away. I watched him walk out of my sight. There was nothing—only emptiness where he had been, only meadow and sky.

Only emptiness! Why was my life like that? I vowed never to place my trust in man again. My mother had trusted the man at the station, she had handed her treasure to him—my mind raced forward, unable to dwell on that darkness. I had trusted my Petur, I had trusted Elder Thorderson—even Father seemed able to fail me for the first time in his life. No one is ever really there when you need them. I had learned that before. Why had I forgotten?

I would not forget again. There was no one. No one in life but yourself you can count upon. What a desolate thought! But I hugged it to me, for there was nothing else I could think of to comfort me.

Chapter Thirteen

The week after Elder Thorderson left us a letter came through the mails from Petur. It was postmarked New York. Just the sight of his name, written in his own hand, sent a strange thrill through me. He was alive after all; he was real again!

Father opened the letter slowly. I thought for a moment he might not read it out loud—might not read it at all. After long minutes he handed it over to Mother.

"Read it, Margret."

"I think Anna ought to do that."

I snatched it eagerly out of her hand. "Dear Father—Dear Father, Mother and Family," it began.

It wasn't, after all, really much of a letter. He told us he was safe and well.

"I was robbed in Missouri," he wrote. "But I have been lucky. I have always found work to do and ways to get on. I have booked passage on a ship that will take me to Iceland. *Enterprise* is her name. She sails the first week of August. By the time you receive this letter I may already be gone."

I glanced at the postmark. It was dated two months ago. What had happened to Petur since then? His closing sentence was not easy for me to read. I stared down at the page, not wanting to see my father's face.

"There is much," Petur wrote, "to see and learn here. But there is no one to love. I do love you all. I hope this finds you well and safe. Love, Petur."

There was silence for a moment. Then my father said in a voice that was not his voice, "There is love, and then there is love." I took the paper that had been folded in with the letter and handed it to him. He handed it to my mother. She opened it slowly and drew out a crisp, twenty-dollar bill. My father made a sound far back in his throat and shook his head. An expression that was almost a smile passed over my mother's features.

"There is a note folded in with the money, Einar. It says, 'I know you will not want to take this, Father. But I earned it by hard, honest labor. That, if nothing else about me, you can't disapprove.' "

I think my father would have thrown the bill into the fire, but my mother rose from her chair and took bill, paper, and letter and put them in the jar high up on her kitchen shelf.

"Enough of all this for now," she said in a voice of no non-sense. Then more softly, under her breath, "Thank heaven he is safe." I was happy to whisper amen to that. My father, with a deep sigh, rose from his chair.

"Well, Margret, there is work that wants doing. I'll see you at supper."

"See that you do," she called after him. "No more forgetting and working straight through, you hear?"

I watched him walk away. His body was thin still, the line of his shoulders stooping. I didn't like that. I could hear my mother at work in the kitchen. She was humming a tune. I couldn't remember the last time I had heard her do that.

The Saints are great ones to celebrate. Any occasion that can offer the least excuse they will latch upon. In Spanish Fork was gathered a conglomeration of people from points all over the

world. Thus we celebrated Robbie Burns Day for the Scotsmen in
January, St. David's Day for the Welsh March 1, St. Patrick's Day
two weeks later for sake of the Irish, even August 2 was noted for
the sake of the few Icelanders who held their Independence Day
sacred. But the culmination came in July with the celebration of
American independence and Pioneer Day all at once.

Spanish Fork was a part of the Provo Stake then, and this year
Pioneer Day was well attended. It seemed all of Spanish Fork
turned out in their wagons to drive the distance to Provo. I wanted
to go and was glad when my mother convinced my father that we
all needed a season of rest, however brief it might be. Though rest
was not the right word, really. We cooked and scrubbed and
cleaned for days before, just to be ready for a brief celebration of a
few hours' duration. Life is like that. But I didn't really mind. I
hungered for distraction and gaiety.

Many families left the night before and camped over. We left
early on the day, before it was light. I wanted to see the parade in
the morning. I had heard about such parades but had never seen
them: the brass bands, the marching girls in white dresses, flags
waving and the firing of cannon, music, and men on horseback
with banners waving.

We arrived in time for the men on horseback, the banners and
speeches, but we missed the first part of the day when the cannons
were fired and the young girls marched through the streets in
white dresses with wreaths festooning their heads. I had wanted to
see that. I should have liked to have been one of those girls.

But all disappointment left me when I recognized the man who
had risen to speak. He was not tall, but his manner was kingly. His
shoulders were broad; he looked sturdy and sure. And his eyes,
though I could not see them directly, seemed to reach out and
pierce every person there. I had felt those blue-gray eyes meet my
own eyes. I had heard that voice speak kind words to me!

I tried hard to pay heed to the words he was speaking as well
as to the man himself.

It was observed this morning that the government of the United
States was the best or most wholesome one on the earth. The signers
of the Declaration of Independence and the framers of the Constitution were inspired from on high to do that work. It was the voice

of the Lord inspiring all those worthy men who bore influence in those trying times . . .

I listened. I had not expected to hear this, to feel the outpouring of love from this prophet as he paid tribute to the country he loved and believed in.

This government, so formed, has been blessed by the Almighty —

Would I ever share these feelings he had for America?

We mean to sustain the Constitution of the United States and all righteous laws. If we live our religion, honor our God and his Priesthood, then we shall honor every wholesome government and law there is upon the earth.

He would understand about Iceland; I knew it — about the majesty of our laws and our history.

I say God speed everybody that is for freedom and equal rights! I am with you.

On and on he went. I had quite forgotten the power he had to get into my heart. He swept me along with the force of his own emotions. These moments for me were hallowed. But hallowed moments were never meant to come more than betwixt and between, brief glimmers set out from the gray and the ordinary. I didn't take Brigham Young's words past their first level, into the dimension of myself, at least not at this time. But I clapped with the others until my palms stung and sang the songs till my throat was dry, and ate the good food and enjoyed the company. And then I saw him.

It was late in the afternoon. The crowds had thinned out some. There was still dancing and singing planned, and some Welshmen, dressed in their native costumes, were among the entertainers. He was there, brightly colored like all the others. He was there with his wide, warm grin, his brown hair in his eyes, and a pretty Welsh girl with her arm wound through his, her eyes sparkling and dancing.

All the food I had eaten so happily soured my stomach. I thought I might really get ill; I felt weak in the head. How could one moment, one sight spoil all happiness for me? Owen moved away with the rest, the girl still beside him. Why couldn't the earth just open and swallow me up?

My father at last had relaxed. He was not eager to load the wagon and go. That meant we would be staying for the last of the entertainment, which included Welsh dancers, Welsh singing and poetry.

When Owen came on I was drawn, in spite of myself, to watch him. His natural exuberant air had a polish to it. A dignified choir of men had performed before. But he danced with the young people, the girl on his arm. I tried to picture myself in her place as I watched him, to feel the press of his hand on my waist, his fingers in mine, his eyes lighting sparks in my own.

When the dancing was over one lone woman walked out onto the cleared, open-air stage. She was dressed in a simple white gown with no other adornment. Close beside her was placed a small harp of exquisite design and a stool for the harpist to sit on. The watchers grew quiet. A sense of expectation ran through the air. Then *he* came. He walked out all alone. He had shed his bright colors, dressed now in modest fawn pants and white shirt with sleeves that billowed in the light evening breeze as the woman's dress billowed.

He sat down on the stool by the harp. His fingers touched it. Lovingly—I could feel that from where I stood. He leaned slightly forward. The audience leaned with him. He ran the tips of his fingers along the strings and the magic began.

The woman sang a song and the harp sang with her. Owen leaned back and closed his eyes.

> Come again this evening, birds of Rhiannon,
> Sing us a song from o'er the blue wave—

My heart caught in my throat at the loveliness of it.

> The smiles on our faces will reveal our hearts' gladness,
> After long grief and affliction grave.

The woman's sweet voice ceased, but the harp kept singing till gently, trembling, the strains grew fainter, then rose with new strength on a swell of air, on a whisper of wind, and a new song moved them, and the woman's voice rose to match them:

Hardd yw Conwy, hardd yw Nefyn—

What was this? What words in what strange tongue?

Hardd yw brigau coedydd Mostyn,
Harddaf lle'r wy'n allu 'nabod

Strange and wild were the words and the music lit them:

Yn y byd yw dyffryn Meifod.

What did they mean? These were the words Owen grew up speaking; this was his own native tongue. It was nothing like mine. Did he love it the way I loved my Icelandic? He leaned with the force of the music, his short frame graceful, the sun finding gold in his hair and along the harp strings.

Un yn gynnes am ei charu,
A'r llall yn oer rhag ofn ei cholli.

The woman's voice grew silent. The harp echoed the last of her song and fell silent, too. Silence hung on the very air, then the crowd erupted with swell after swell of sound. Owen blinked his eyes open, returning with stunned reluctance. My own words came: *What do you take to? What is it you like?*

He turned to the watchers, aware at last of their presence. His beautiful smile began lifting the sides of his mouth. "I like music. . . . I'd like—well, someday I'll tell you." What secrets there were locked up in his sturdy frame! What beauty which I did not know.

I felt fed, replenished. And yet at the same time empty, aching for more.

Chapter Fourteen

Often in those early days of August I thought of Petur. Was he still at sea? Had he even left yet? When would he reach my island? In my mind I would imagine the reunion of grandson and grandfather. I pictured it always on the stretch of rocky sand that held so much of us—our histories, our hearts, our old beginnings.

Perhaps Petur would be happy back home in Iceland, in spite of what Father had said. I knew my grandfather would rejoice in his quiet way to set eyes again on the grandson who was so like his own lost child, to wrap his arms around flesh of his flesh, to hear words spoken in a voice whose tones were familiar and dear.

Summer seemed to slip through our fingers. By the middle of August our new house was ready to roof. And a real roof it would have, too, not just mud and willow. South of town Brother Gardner had built a new sawmill that could make shingles for the roof. There was so much building! Some of the families who had come from Salt Lake to escape Johnston's army decided to stay here and settle. I couldn't believe that. I would still have preferred going back to the city. Who would choose Spanish Fork on purpose? But they came and they stayed, boosting the population to nearly a thousand Saints in our little town. And Johnston's army marched through Salt Lake City as agreed by Brigham Young, not molesting a blade of grass as they passed through, and the tragedy we had all feared was averted. So people breathed freely again and planted their fields and built houses, and the hum of progress was a sound you could almost hear.

We were part of it all, I suppose, though we didn't feel it. You don't feel that kind of thing, you just plod along, more aware of the work and struggle than of the progress, more consumed with the little frustrations than with the victories.

In the last days of August we went back to Provo again. Most of our Spanish Fork families went there together and camped for three days while we harvested manna. There was no store-bought sugar to be found in the settlements. What there was sold in Salt Lake for a dollar a pound. There were very few other ways we could sweeten things. But that summer, along the river bottoms near Provo, a sticky substance was found on the leaves of the trees. It was a simple enough process to gather the leaves there, soak the substance off in water, and boil it down to a thick and satisfactory brown sugar. The people called it manna and some believe it was a sign of divine intervention on behalf of the Saints.

I appreciated the respite from regular labor and the chance to obtain the sweet substance. But that was overshadowed by my disappointment at missing Owen. He was not there. I suspected that he had stayed home to work for his father. I knew Brother Davies had bought a new stretch of ground very near our own bench lands where the soil was adapted to the growing of fruits and fruit trees. He had planted a little orchard of cherries and peaches. I had heard my father say that whoever owned that orchard would have his hands full. It was Owen's hands that were full, and my days seemed empty without sight of him at all, without my Petur, without Elder Thorderson, forever.

Our last day in Provo Father drove with some of the other men into the city. There were a few supplies he wanted to purchase there. He came home with a loaded wagon and, tucked in his armpit, a copy of an eastern newspaper, well read through. Such treasures were rare. What a treat it would be to sit down by the fire and devour every word on the long printed pages!

He seemed strangely quiet, my father. He called us together in a circle outside the wagon. I knew from his eyes that something was very much the matter. He drew out the paper and opened it up on his knees. He cleared his throat once, and looking down at the paper he read out loud:

American liner *Enterprise* sailing Sunday out of New York was last night reported lost two days out on the high seas. Exact location of the sunken vessel is not known. We will furnish more details as they are reported. She carried a crew and passengers totaling 315 people. At this date it is believed there are no survivors.

No survivors . . . the vessel *Enterprise* . . . "I will be sailing . . ." I looked up at my father, and this time he looked at me.

"He is my son," he said. "For some reason I do not believe he is dead, I do not feel it."

We knelt down on the ground there together and prayed for Petur. When we arose my father's face looked relaxed, refreshed.

"Father, if Petur is alive, he will still go to Iceland."

"I know that, Anna," he said. "I have struggled, but in my struggles I have thought first of myself—my pain, my shame, Anna—even my failure in raising a son who would turn his back on his father's religion."

His arm went about my shoulder. I could feel the strength of it. He began walking and I walked with him, trying to move with his stride.

"I did the same thing to my own father, you know. Isn't that how he and the others would see it?"

I nodded. My eyes had grown wide. My father pointed off to the distant mountains that ringed the valley.

"How many years did it take the Creator to make such a wonder as that?"

I smiled at him. I remembered this conversation and tears clouded my eyes.

"A long time," I answered him. "Even for God."

"To create an eternal soul, now, how long would that take?"

I wanted to hug him. "A little longer"—my voice sounded shaky—"than twenty years."

There were tears in my father's eyes now. He swallowed and nodded. "I, who judge no other man, have sinned terribly, Anna. I have judged my own son, I have—"

"Don't, Father! Because you loved him so much he had power to hurt you—more than all other men put together—"

"Oh yes. And I had the same power, Anna, to hurt him as well. I who was meant to be guide and mentor, example and—"

"Father, you were, you are! Don't make it worse by judging yourself. You can't help Petur by making your own life wretched!"

A faint, sad smile crossed his face like a moving shadow. "My wise little Anna. What would I do without you?"

I didn't feel wise. Since the last days of school and my friendship with Owen I had felt awkward and foolish and self-centered. Elder Thorderson's farewell had just added to that.

But as we walked back to the wagon together I knew I had helped him. My heart soared to know I had power to do him good. "Father . . . daughter," he had once said, "that's what we're here for, to help each other along."

At that time I had failed him and added to his pain. But today I had helped to lift the great weight of his burden. For that my heart sang out with joy.

Chapter Fifteen

I had not really meant to honor my promise, the promise Elder Thorderson had extracted from me. But Brother Palsson gave me no peace; he would constantly plague me.

"We need your voice in the choir, Anna; you mustn't refuse. You would be a boon to the women's section. Magnus Thorderson told me not to give up till I had you singing."

So what could I do? And if the truth be known, I needed diversion, something to tempt my thoughts away from the fate of my brother and the emptiness of my own life.

I started singing. Twice a week we would gather to practice. At first it was hard. I had always sung by myself, with nobody to hear me. Now I must discipline my voice to the tone of the group, be listened to, take instruction and criticism. But I could feel both my voice and my confidence growing. And once I relaxed a little and gave in to the song, the melody soothed my spirit and healed and fed it. Oh, the wild, sweet songs of my homeland! I soon looked forward to those sessions as to the very core of my life, my reason for being.

August hovered and lingered; I scarcely noticed when she slipped aside for September. The days went on. We heard no additional news about Petur or the fate of the sailing ship *Enterprise*. My birthday came with September and so did the marking of the first year since our arrival in the land of the Saints. In August a year ago we had reached Salt Lake City. On my birthday, September 10, we had awakened here, in the melting pot of Utah. One year ago. This was home for weak or strong, for good or ill. Iceland was only a dream. I was nineteen years old. Too old to go to school. I convinced my mother, but my father was not so easy. At last he agreed to allow me to study independently with my teacher. This study would prepare me for serious courses if the opportunity happened to come. Could my gentle father hold the same hopes for me that I held in my own heart?

A new pattern began to emerge. I spent my mornings helping Mother with whatever work there was to be done. In the afternoons I would read from the list of books my teacher provided and prepare the lessons she outlined for me. I liked the work. If the lessons seemed to go well I rewarded my efforts with an hour of reading Icelandic. One evening each week and early on Saturday mornings I sang with the choir. Other than that I had no social interaction, save meeting times on Sunday, and those didn't count. I had no friends to speak of, but I was happy. Lonely at times, sometimes discontented, but happier in my own world than in any other.

Work on the house progressed and I helped my father—sometimes in place of working for my mother, sometimes in place of my studies or even my rest. But I was happiest, really, when working beside him. He seemed at peace with himself once more. Of course, the pain was still there in his eyes sometimes. But I felt I had the father I knew and loved restored to me again.

One Saturday morning our choir director dismissed us early. There was still song bubbling up inside me. I walked to the hills, not my own familiar stretch, but the steep outcroppings that sat above Olaffsons' house where our practice was held. The September shades of color were still a dim promise. But I could smell autumn in the wind and excitement swept through me, and a vague, restless longing. I sat on the hilltop and sang for the wind to hear, and the trees sang with me. I closed my eyes to immerse my whole soul in the sound. It was the most perfect, unself-conscious moment I can remember.

I opened my eyes to find him standing there, watching. Owen's blue eyes were round as marbles, his mouth was soft. I wanted the earth to swallow me. He said very softly, "Anna, I had no idea you sang like that."

I made a small noise back in my throat. He kept looking at me. "Do you come here often?" he asked.

"No, no. Not at all."

"Not at all?"

"Well, they let our practice out early. I decided to walk up here for a while." My cheeks were burning. The old haltness had bitten my tongue.

"What practice?"

"I sing with the Icelandic choir," I explained.

"For how long?" His eyes had grown bright with interest.

"I don't know. A few months," I said.

"I sing in a choir. It's a community choir—" He laughed. "A Welsh choir, I guess, since Brother Jones organized it and most of the singers are Welsh—but I don't sing like that."

I looked down at his kind words. "I'm sorry, Anna. You embarrass easily, don't you? Or maybe it's me. I do have a talent for blundering . . ."

I couldn't help smiling. "You have a talent for making music with more than your voice."

He liked that. His grin started breaking. "I guess I do. I love music—"

"I know. You once told me that. But you didn't tell me you played the harp."

His grin grew wider. "You heard me play on Pioneer Day?"

I nodded, trying to blur the image of the pretty girl that rose up in my mind.

"The harp you saw me playing? I made that!"

"You made an instrument, a harp?"

"With my own two hands—from a beautiful block of wood. It took months to fashion—"

"And the carving—did you do the carvings?"

"Of course I did."

"I had no idea. My father would love to examine those carvings."

"I'll bring it by some time. Does your father work with wood?"

"He loves to. And he's good. But he's never done something that fine."

Owen sat down on a rock by my feet and stretched out his legs. "It's a skill I learned as a child. I have an old uncle back home who taught me. It's been handed down since—well, since long before our history was known and recorded."

I thought of the precious things handed down in my culture. It was like that with Owen as well, but I could not imagine, could not picture the things that were priceless to him.

"Did your uncle teach you to play the harp after you made it?"

He laughed softly. "Oh, no, an old witch-woman taught me that."

I sat up and he laughed out loud at the look on my face. "Don't Icelanders believe in the fairy folk? I suppose not. I'm sure it's much too cold in Iceland for the fairies' liking."

"And just what do you know about Iceland?" The words were a tease.

"I know it grows the prettiest girls I've seen. Isn't that enough, now?"

"More than enough!" How lovely he was to talk with!

He pushed back his mop of brown hair. "I've missed you, Anna. Where have you been keeping yourself?"

"I've been around. It's you who's been in hiding all summer."

"That's true enough. I've been slave to my father's orchard. Nurse to a crop of new trees." He made his face pucker into a picture of mocking distress. "I'm glad to learn that you noticed— perhaps you missed me."

"Perhaps."

"Oh, Anna, it's so good to see you again! But I must be off now. Father will miss me and be in a fury." He tipped his cap, winked one mischievous eye, and left me so quickly that the dust seemed to swirl on the spot where his feet had last stood.

I shook my head. *What a strange boy, Owen.* I walked slowly back home, but my mind was disturbed, and the peace of the day was shattered for me.

The next choir practice was held Wednesday night. I attended as usual. But for some reason I found it difficult concentrating. My mind kept wandering. What was Owen doing? What songs did his choir sing? Would he like this music, this song we were working on now? When I thought about it I remembered that there was a choir in Spanish Fork. They had even performed now and then at some public function. But I had never paid much attention before.

Now the word *choir* meant only one thing: *Owen. Music* meant only the lilt in his voice and the sigh of his harp.

When the practice was dismissed I felt vaguely restless. I hated the idea of merely walking home, going to bed. But what else could I possibly do? I looked up at the hillside. It was already swathed in shadow with pockets of black filling in the crevices, hiding the hollows. There was no hope of walking there. And I didn't want to. I wanted something I couldn't quite name or define.

I turned down the street and, of course, I did not hear him. I had never heard him yet. He came up beside me. "I know another place we can walk. Would you like to?"

"Very much." A tingling sensation crept over my skin. "Did your choir practice this evening, too?"

He grinned gently at me. "No. Only Saturday mornings."

"Then—"

"I have my ways, Anna. Saturday morning was much too short for my liking. There was so much I still wanted to talk about."

And we talked. We sat down on a log where a stream wound, silent and silver beside our feet. We threw stones across it. We watched a boy bring his father's cows in from pasture. We watched the moon rise, a soft golden orb in a lavender sky. We watched the first stars that came with the moon. These weren't the shy ones, but the bold, bright, splendid jewels, so sure of their place, so eager to be admired.

"It's hard to imagine that these stars shine over my Iceland."

He looked at me. "It's a long way away, that's for sure. So is my land. But I was much younger when I left, and I wanted to come. You didn't want to come much, did you, Anna?"

"I didn't want to *leave*. It was more that way."

He nodded. "It was hard back in Wales, that much I remember. I watched my father work twelve hours in the mine every day—it was as if he lived there. Only Sundays was he home. And of course in the evenings. Most days he never saw the sun."

"Iceland wasn't like that. We worked hard to keep alive, but we had our pleasures. And so much beauty. And peace, and song."

"We had pleasures, too, but they tasted bitter—layered with

coal dust, I guess." He laughed softly. "Anyway, that's all behind us. This is a new land and I, for one, like it here."

"I'm glad." I said the words quietly.

He leaned closer to me, peering squint-eyed into my face. "You're much like my mother. You hang on so tightly. I think you're afraid to let go."

He could see that his words upset me. With a deft move he changed the subject. "That song you were singing—what's it called? I liked it."

I told him the name and he grinned. "You sing in Icelandic. Do you pray and think in Icelandic?"

"Sometimes. The girl who sang with you sang in Welsh, I remember. So why do you criticize me?"

"There you go again, Anna. I don't mean to criticize you, I *tease*. Can't you tell the difference?"

"I guess not." I rose from my seat. "It's getting late now."

"Anna, Anna." He walked by my side, still shaking his head. "You are quite a puzzle, Anna. When shall I come over?"

I looked at him sharply.

"And show your father my harp?"

He really meant to come! "Let me ask him about it." A flood of fears assailed me.

"All right. In time, then." He walked me all the way through town to the edge of the bench line.

"I can make it from here," I said.

He peered up at the uneven lights that hugged the cliffside. "Little Iceland." His voice was thoughtful. "I'll walk all the way."

"I don't think you ought to." I shook my head.

"Don't worry, Anna. Surely nothing can come from my walking you home." He took my arm in the darkness. I let him guide me. His touch was warm against my flesh. Everything about Owen was warm and alive and pulsing. He was never downhearted. He never seemed to tire, to fear, to doubt.

"What are you thinking about, Anna?"

I gulped in the darkness.

"All right, you don't have to tell me. But someday I shall get it from you!" We reached my door. It seemed much too soon. He let my arm drop.

"Goodbye, Anna Jonsson. I shall see you again."

He turned and walked into the darkness. I could hear him whistling, a stream of silver music winding down through the night. I opened the door and walked into the house. Would my parents notice the bloom of his words and his laugh on my cheeks?

Maybe Father did notice something. He seemed to stare at me, to give me a long, searching look.

"You are late getting home."

Of course! I hadn't once thought about it. I would have to give some explanation.

"I went for a walk."

"With the young man who was at the door?"

"Yes, Father."

I took my shawl off and hung it on the peg beside Mother's. It seemed that my fingers were trembling. Was Father still watching me?

"Was it a nice walk? What is the young man's name?" It was my mother's voice asking the questions. What did it matter?

I took a deep breath. "Owen Davies. I know him from school."

"Isn't he the Welsh boy who didn't join in the trouble that time with Petur?"

How had my father remembered?

"Yes, Father. He's a nice boy. I just . . . happened to meet him—" That was the truth. At least from my side of the matter. My father nodded. He seemed satisfied for the moment. My mother frowned and began to fuss with a knot in her thread. For a moment I wondered if I should say something about the harp. But I didn't think so. Not now. Not yet. I walked back to my bed. Why had my mother frowned? Her frown was a shadow to dull the brightness of the night and of Owen's smile.

I knelt down to say my prayers. The words came in English. That surprised me a little. But I thought I may as well finish in English. The words felt good. If Owen knew I was praying in English he would laugh at me. The thought gave me a sense of pleasure. I shook my head and forced Owen Davies out of my mind.

Chapter Sixteen

Saturday came, but there was no choir practice. A storm had been threatening for days and the fields were burdened with harvest that must be gathered. All activity ceased except that which was most expedient. I was unhappy. I missed singing, but more than that I wondered: Would Owen have been there to meet me? I wanted to know. Would he miss not seeing me there? Or was he too busy, too immersed in his work for vague thoughts of me?

The whole week went on in that pattern and, though I was busy, I wasn't busy enough to drive thought from my mind or longing from my heart. Once the harvest was gathered the work to prepare and preserve the food fell to women's hands. The Saints had just passed through a period of near-starvation. In '56 potatoes were selling for three dollars a bushel and flour for ten. Our family had arrived at the tail end of these troubles. As the Saints began to pull out and the crops improve, they would harvest the wheat as individual patches ripened: cut it, dry it, and thresh it out with a flail. The cool morning winds that poured down from the canyon blew away the chaff as the wheat was poured from the pan. Of course, after that the wheat was ground by hand into flour. Even then there were greens and fish to augment our diet. Now the crops were doing well, and the grateful who gathered worked with almost a sense of reverence. Brother Gardner's flour mill was still far from completion. It was providing work for men such as my father, but no help for the women as yet.

Work on our own house during this period came to a standstill. My father had only two hands and so many hours. Samuel was now strong enough to help him; for that I was grateful. For my mother's work had multiplied during the harvest and she had need of me every minute that I could spare.

But the Indian summer days hovered and lingered. Inside work on the house could be done when the weather turned poor. So could book work and, apparently, so could singing.

A week, two weeks passed since I had last seen Owen. The days merged into one another until I lost track of time. The dried meat and corn, the jars on the preserves shelf, the potatoes in the cellar, all attested to the work of our busy hands.

One mild day in October Mother was called to Brother Sveinsson's house. His young wife, Freyja, had gone into labor the night before. This would be their first child. There was a regular midwife in Spanish Fork now, but she had gone into Payson on a case. The Sveinssons felt comfortable calling Mother; she was happy to go. Quite happy, in fact, for this chance to rest from those labors which had held her to such strict routine for the past several weeks.

"You come, too," she said to me as she gathered her things up. "We will let the kitchen fires rest for a day. Bring Gesli and Sina. They can play in the meadows behind the house."

I knew the Sveinsson place. Though there now were orchards, rows of small spindly trees such as Owen's father's, the Sveinssons boasted one of the few real fruit trees in the valley—a peach tree planted from a pit brought by Brigham Young! It stood now nearly four feet high and its small crop of peaches were as delicious as the legendary ambrosia; I had tasted one. They boasted also a row of cottonwood trees at the edge of the meadow, trees they had carried on their backs from the Provo river bottoms and planted carefully one by one. They provided some shade and a sweet sense of privacy. I was eager to go there, to catch my breath, to play with the children.

As we walked along single file little Sina tugged at Mother's shawl insistently. "What is it, child?" Mother disliked being pestered. She thought frontier children much more poorly behaved than the children in Iceland.

"Will the Indians be there?"

I had nearly forgotten! Indians often camped on the Sveinssons' land. He was good to them: his wife would feed them, he would listen to their complaints against the white men, and often, to quiet their disgruntled resentment, give them the animals they picked out and demanded. I knew Sina was frightened, but I was curious to see some of these Lamanites at close quarters. I seldom did. I hoped there might be a group there now.

I was not disappointed. About fifteen lodges of the Uintah band were camped in the far meadow. When we entered the house I was full of questions I intended to ask, but my mother hushed me and put me to work at once. She instructed Gesli to watch Sina and stay away from the Indian camp. Then as further guarantee she assigned him his own tasks: things to borrow from one neighbor or another, a purchase to be made in town, small kindling to chop. I stared at the Indians from a frustrated distance only.

They were so different from anything else I had seen here, their ways so alien to the white man's. The manner of their dress, the way they ate and prepared food, their stories and legends, their mannerisms—even their way of walking—seemed strangely reminiscent of home to me. When my mother at last, in exasperation, called me away from the window and pulled the curtain, I couldn't help speaking out loud my observation.

"The Indians look as though they'd be quite at home in Iceland, Mother."

"Yes, they do. I've always thought that."

I looked up, surprised. She smiled. "Don't appear so amazed, Anna. I am as free to observe as you. I have often watched them and felt sorry for their confusion. The white man's ways will never feel right to them. On the Westmann Islands they would still hear the spirits and feel the peace they would cling to here."

It was the longest speech I can remember my mother making. I felt warm as I listened to her. Perhaps we shared other feelings, other opinions, without even knowing.

I watched her work through the rest of the day with an added respect, an added edge of interest.

Freyja Sveinsson's baby was a beautiful girl with down-soft hair like fluff on the top of her head and behind her ears. She smelled as sweet as new spring rain or wild summer roses. I had never been so near to a birth before. I could understand for the first time my mother's fascination—the exhilaration she felt, the wonder and joy.

I had almost forgotten the Indians when at last we started for home; I was so exhausted. It was dark and the meadow was bathed in shadow. The lodges loomed as large bulky shadows interspersed here and there, looking ungainly and out of place in the smooth line of meadow. Perhaps Mother would come back tomorrow and help young Freyja and I could come with her again and sneak closer this time. I'm sure Sina didn't feel the same way; she clung tight to my fingers and made her body arch away from the closer shadows that stretched themselves out before us. Not so Gesli. He ran ahead in quick, darting spurts, wandering off the pathway to explore some strange noise or shape as a half-grown puppy would do. I watched him, almost wishing I could be like him, could command half his store of energy.

We walked on for a few moments in tired silence until I realized suddenly Gesli was nowhere to be seen. There were no breathless exclamations, no spatter of footsteps. No noise at all. We stopped still where we stood. I dreaded to call him. I had called out once before for a child—

A screech owl cried like a frightened animal; Sina cried in answer. I tightened my hold on her hand. The echoes faded. Nothing but silence again.

"Do you think the Indians have him, Anna?"

"Hush, Sina." I spoke roughly to cover my fear. "Of course not. He forgot all about us in following something interesting he discovered." My words did nothing at all to comfort my fears.

At last Mother cupped her hands and called loudly. Nothing. We waited a moment. I could not bear waiting. I took a few steps to the side of the road. The tall meadow grasses were choked here with brambly bushes and a small stand of box elders. There was probably water nearby. I walked a bit further. The ground gave to my steps too easily; the shadows were deep here. Was there water just steps away? Should I attempt going further?

I drew a deep breath and tried to think calmly. The sound was a shadow, as eerie and insubstantial as those at my feet. I froze. The sound came again. I knew it. As crazy as it seemed, the sound took shape and pierced into my skull.

"Anna! Anna!"

Gesli—I knew it was Gesli. I stumbled forward. I must have called out his name. My mother followed. Then suddenly she was past me and onto the ground, the hem of her skirt soaked and dragging mud.

"What is it?" I heard myself ask.

Gesli touched the bundle. "I think—" His voice was still shadow. "I think it's a baby."

My first thought was of Owen's fairies; I shrank back a little. Mother bent lower. She scooped up the form and held it carefully to her.

"We can see nothing here. Let's find the road, Anna."

Gesli held to the hem of her skirt and I guided Sina. We went slowly. It seemed to take us a very long time. Once back on the firm stretch of road I felt much, much safer. It had been easy to picture eyes peering through the bushes and long grass, to hear in the insects' scratching and the crunch of our own steps the soft tread of mocassined warriors.

"Where are you going?" My mother had turned around, heading back to the house. I followed her with reluctance.

"We must see what we have here." There was a quality to her voice which I couldn't place. We knocked on the Sveinssons' door and were quickly admitted. Brother Sveinsson looked at the bundle my mother carried and raised his brow.

"Where did you find this, Sister Jonsson?"

She told him. He listened intently, nodding now and again, but his eyes looked troubled.

"It is an Indian child abandoned for some good reason."

"Good reason?"

Brother Sveinsson shrugged his shoulders, as though to say, "Don't ask me to explain." "It is hard to guess at," he said. "Perhaps the child's mother has died, or has no milk to feed it. Sometimes a child refuses to eat and they think it possessed. Or at times—if a child is deformed—" He glanced quickly at Mother. "They will leave it in a ditch or roadside. It is their way."

"They just leave the child there till it dies?" I had to ask it.

"Yes," This was hard for Svein Sveinsson, too. He was partial to the Indians, and close by him, in a soft feather bed, lay his own dear child.

"It was thus in the early days of Iceland," my mother reminded. "When an infant was born it was laid upon the bare ground until the father came to examine his child, see if the lungs were strong and the limbs firmly formed. Not until then was the little one's fate decided."

Brother Sveinsson raised his eyebrows again. "Well," he said with his hand on the blanket, "let's see what we've got here."

That was just what my mother had said. He drew back the cover. At first it was hard to see what was in there. I leaned closer.

I could make out a small round face with tiny puckered lips, very delicate features, nose and ears. Gesli pulled at the cover. The baby had thick black hair that grew over its earlobes—handfuls of silken hair. I reached out a finger.

Mother examined the baby carefully, inch by inch. I realized as I watched I was holding my breath. "If a child is deformed . . ." Mother turned her all over. It was a baby girl, we discovered. Little Sina was smiling.

"She's beautiful, Mother," she breathed.

My mother said nothing. She examined the child once again. There seemed nothing, nothing. I rubbed her soft cheek with my finger; her hand closed around it. The baby cooed and smiled. I looked up at my mother. She looked again at the hands and the child's tiny feet. Perfect.

"I think this child was born early," she said. "Perhaps she cannot suck well. Is there some way to find where she came from?"

Brother Sveinsson shook his head. "No, no, you do not understand. This child is abandoned. No one wants it. No one will take it back."

"Then . . ." I let the word hang in the air. I kept watching my mother.

"There are various things you can do, Sister Jonsson. Take the child to the Indian agent here—that is one."

"What would happen then?" I asked.

"It would not be pleasant. Would be much better to find someone to care for the child. A white family who would raise the girl up with their own."

"Just like that? No inquiries, no arrangements?"

"Sister Jonsson—to her Indian people this child is dead."

My mother closed her eyes. I knew what she was thinking, knew what she was seeing inside her head. *Just like that a child disappears—just like that a baby found in the bushes, like a kitten, becomes your own.*

At last my mother opened her eyes. "We will take the infant. We will take her home with us. It will be all right."

I squeezed little Sina's hand. She smiled at me.

"I shall harness the horse to the wagon."

"No, don't do that. We can be home before it is ready."

Mother tucked in the blankets and covered the pretty round face against the night air. Understanding, I picked up her bags and bundles. She nestled the child against her. We walked out of the house and to our home in a dreamlike silence, as rich as the silence at meetings or moments of prayer.

Chapter Seventeen

Mother named the little girl Haldora, after her own mother. I thought it a lovely name. When Freyja Sveinsson discovered what had happened the night her own daughter was born, she offered to suckle the infant along with hers. It was an answer to all our prayers, especially Mother's. Haldora thrived on the young mother's milk, put on flesh and grew rosy. For weeks then it seemed Mother lived at the Sveinssons, traipsing there several times a day with the hungry baby. Eventually we began supplementing with goats' milk, but at first I took over more and more of her duties as Mother devoted herself to the care of the child. Haldora thrived on more than rich milk—she thrived on our love. And we basked in the love she returned to us.

Samuel fished with a basket trap back of the dam and worked at the harvest, taking Gesli with him to pit his budding skill with a rifle against the plucky wild ducks that infested the farmers' fields. Grouse and prairie chicken, too, made excellent eating. Gesli took seriously his role as hunter and did well for a boy his age. For the first time ever he had some way to really contribute, a work of his own.

Sweet Sina. She was the one who blossomed. In the care of the Indian child she forgot herself. More than that, she had something to love again, someone to love her. How empty her heart must have been before!

My father's joy was in watching my mother, which he did with extreme discretion. She and the child were part of the self-same miracle. Father observed it, being as tender with both as a man could be, but loving Haldora, I believe, less in her own right than in gratitude for the happiness she brought to his Margret.

On the last golden day of October we cleared out the dugout, loaded all our things into the wagon, and said goodbye to the plain, simple shelter which had been home to us all.

It was harder than I had expected to leave it behind me. So many memories were crammed into that small space. The empty rooms of the new house seemed huge and unfriendly. There would be glass in the windows there, though not for some time yet, and space to expand the three rooms into more. It would be a lovely house; Father's touch was on it. I said goodbye to the dugout and felt in my heart I would be leaving my childhood behind — and Petur, too. The house we were going to had no memories, no knowledge of him. It was a new house for a new family. With Haldora here we were more a family than ever. But still, Petur was missing. Would the day ever come when I forgot to notice his absence with pain?

Busy days, but happy days. Only one thing disturbed me. We had moved just a short distance away, but the hill behind me had a character of its own; it was not my hill. The stones, the dips and hollows, the bushes that grew there, the color of sky and grass — they meant nothing to me. I was not part of them yet. I longed for my own spot, so intimately familiar, so suited to me.

The days smoothed out a little; I felt I could breathe now. I found myself studying again, and for more than snatched minutes. Gesli went to school with Samuel once the harvest was finished, and Sina helped with the baby. I found my days with time in them again for myself.

I didn't take to the hillside until a morning of fine rain and mist that drew longing from me, that called to my restless spirit. I grabbed a warm shawl and headed up the gray slope bent on exploring.

Shadow sat well on the hills; the wet grass looked greener than it did on the hot, brittle days. There were one or two trees here, stunted and weathered, but near their roots was a natural hollow, a cranny to sit and dream in.

I couldn't do that today; the wet ground would soak me. I walked on. The clouds had erased the sky. Gray air merged into gray rock; the line of mountain disappeared in the fog that sank down to my feet.

I could taste the rain in the air, cold inside my cheeks. I drew the smell of the sweet rain into my nostrils. The wet leaves on the far, high peaks shone with brilliant color: scarlet and orange and gold, wide stretches of color splashed in bold disarray on the mountains' flanks. I felt poetry well up like music inside me.

"No one but a crazy girl from Iceland would walk out in such weather."

I turned. It could only be him!

"Oh, Owen! What a pleasure to find you here. I have so much to tell you."

I stumbled toward him over the uneven ground. He took my hand and we walked in the mist together, and I told him all that was in my heart—not only about the new house and the Indian baby, but how I felt when we left the dugout, and what it was like when my mother closed her eyes and remembered and feared, and then opened them wide to the need of a child, the demands of love.

He listened. He did more than listen; he felt with me. There were no clever remarks, no gentle teasing. Once or twice he shook his head. "I had no idea! I had no idea!" he mumbled as I hurried on.

At last, when the words were spent, I felt a shyness. What had moved me to open my heart that way? Perhaps he sensed my distress. He stepped closer to me. "What of Petur?" he asked very gently. "How is it with Petur?"

I looked into his kind blue eyes and I told him. I had never told any living person before. When my eyes filled with tears at the telling he drew me to him, and I cried against his shoulder, and it felt right, and I was no longer shy when I moved away from him.

"The earth weeps with you, Anna, and so do I. It is not easy what you've borne, and you've borne it so bravely."

"You've let me cry on your shoulder."

He brushed that off. "I'm grateful I was here for once when you needed me."

He said that with all the warmth of his generous nature. His warmth reached around me, as comforting as his arms had been. The mist thickened into rain; we should have sought cover. But we walked hand in hand, never heeding at all.

The mild days held. The first week of November a dramatic performance was enacted for the community's pleasure. An open-air stage was contrived inside the old fort. If the weather had been bad, the production would have been forced inside, into the schoolhouse. It was so much nicer this way. The drama was entitled *Priestcraft in Danger,* and I knew personally most of the members of the cast, including a certain bright-eyed Welsh boy who played "Theopholus Thundercloud." There were three nights of performance. I missed the first one because both little Haldora and Mother were sick. But Father promised that I could attend the last two performances. The closing night there was to be a party for the cast members, and I was invited — as partner to one of the stars of the cast.

I sat through the play enraptured; I had seen nothing like it. It wasn't quality drama, I know, but oh, it was moving. And Owen performed with his usual enthusiasm, totally unself-conscious. I shared in his mood, knowing I had not that kind of confident bravado inside myself.

I sat with Samuel and Gesli and Sina and when it was over I sent them scampering home and went looking for Owen. He had asked me not to leave without seeing him first. There were crowds of people to push my way through and I was anxious. I nearly stumbled over a mother trailing four children and, seeing no way around it, I stooped to help, pulling the two older ones up by their hands to where their mother might secure them beside her, at least for a while. It was then, while struggling with the children, that I heard the stranger. Otherwise, I would surely have passed him by.

It's a strange thing hearing your name jump out at you — your own name crystallized from a hubbub of words in a hundred voices.

"Einar Jonsson — Anna — Samuel — does anyone know them? They lived in a dugout up on the bench. Yes, yes, Icelanders. No longer there, it seems. Do you know where they might have moved?"

It was a loud, friendly voice. My eyes searched for the owner. He stopped another person to ask. I drew closer to him and tapped him on the shoulder to get his attention.

"Excuse me, sir, I can help you—" He turned with a smile. He was lean and handsome and wore a blonde beard streaked through with red. "I am Anna Jonsson—I am . . ."

He had thrown back his head to laugh. I stared at him. Were my eyes playing tricks on me? I stepped away from him. It could not possibly, possibly be!

He took both my hands, ever so gently, and drew me to him. "Anna, I've given you such a fright. I'm dreadfully sorry. I never meant it to happen this way."

"Petur?"

"Yes, Anna, it is your Petur come home."

Still I did not believe it. I examined him closely. The beard— the beard made a difference. But there was more. He rubbed the skin above his left eye with a slender finger.

"Same scar right here. Remember, Anna, when I sneaked off to spear fish on my tenth birthday? And I can tell you what happened to you on the day you turned twelve and your—"

"Stop, stop!" It must be Petur, but I didn't feel it. He looked into my eyes. "Have I really frightened you, Anna?"

"We all thought you were dead. In an Eastern paper Father read of the wreck of the *Enterprise*—"

"How did he ever get hold of a newspaper like that clear out here? I had no idea. You must have been—Oh, Anna. I blustered in like a cold Northern ghost, all breeched and bearded—" He looked down at himself.

"You look wonderful, Petur. You look like a man."

"It's the beard. Don't let it fool you."

It *was* Petur! "How did you—why is it? . . ."

"How is it that I am alive, standing here before you? Many things have played a part, many miracles, Anna. I'll tell all. But first, will you take me home?"

There was something different. I still felt it. But he was alive and well and *here*. "Hold my hand tightly. If we run, we'll be there in five minutes."

"I'm game."

His hand felt twice as big as the last time I had held it. Broad and sinewy. He could run fast. I held on as tightly as I could and sped along with him.

I walked into the house before him. How could I prepare them? My father looked up from the book he was reading. "You're home early, Anna. How was the performance?"

The performance! Owen! I had completely forgotten. My hand went up to my mouth. My mother came walking in from the back of the house, looking bleary-eyed. "Hush, you two, I just got Haldora sleeping."

I may have stared at her. "Anna, what is it?" she asked.

I ran my hand across my forehead. "I've brought someone home with me. I met him—by accident—after the play. He was looking for our house—" This was really foolish! But what else could I do? "Father, Petur is back."

He walked in, as if on cue. It might have been better if he had given them the space of a breath or two. I don't know how different he looked to their eyes. He stood a moment surveying the room, getting his bearings. Then he walked across to my mother, bent over, and kissed her. She made a little sound and touched his cheek with her hand. He turned and looked straight at Father. From where I stood I could see him. There was no defiance, no fear, nothing dark in his eyes.

"Sir, if you don't wish me to stay . . . well, I'll understand it. I'd just like . . ."

My father was rising from his chair and standing. Petur waited, his eyes filled with something tender.

Father stood straight and tall by his chair. For the first time I noticed that Petur stood just as tall, perhaps taller than Father.

"I never thought to see you again in the flesh, Petur." Father's voice was strong and sure. "My prayers have been answered. Welcome home, son." He held his arms open. Without a word Petur went, buried his head against the lean, strong shoulder, and cried like a little boy.

I looked over at Mother. She motioned and I gratefully followed her into the kitchen. She began pulling out pans and dishes.

"I've never known a man come home from anywhere who isn't hungry, most likely half-starved."

She stirred up the fire. I bent to help her. It was good having work for my hands to do.

We talked late into the night. Or rather, we listened while Petur told the adventures and trials that had filled his life for the past months. They told like a story: Indian attacks, a prairie stampede, river men stealing money and beating a man to death, half a dozen different jobs, all kinds of company, all kinds of living conditions and scenery, and the ship *Enterprise* that sailed without him while he lay tossing with typhoid in a cheap rented room.

"It was there, in that wretched room, when the fever left me, that I read the Book of Mormon from cover to cover." A ghost of a smile played across the lean, bearded features. "There was nothing else to do but lay there and suffer. At first I read just to keep from going mad. Then something happened. I started losing track of the time, of the world, of myself. The landlady who brought my meals complained because I didn't touch her food. How could I get well and out of her way if I didn't eat? she would mumble—with a string of colorful curses for emphasis."

We had come to the heart of the matter. I knew it. I felt myself holding my breath as Petur went on.

"I had nothing but time. When I finished reading I got down on my knees like it tells you to. I don't think I'd ever really prayed until that moment. I knelt there so long I was nearly too weak to get back up. But when I stood on my feet I knew, Father, I *knew* for the very first time—"

There were tears in my eyes. I blinked them away and smiled bravely at Petur.

"Soon as my strength returned I went looking for work so I could pay the landlady."

"What did you do?"

"I worked on the docks unloading cargo. I watched the big ships come in day by day. I watched the sailors. Every kind of creature on the earth seemed to pass through that port." He shuddered, and I wondered what it was he remembered.

"I made my plans and, once I had earned all the money I needed, I set my face toward home." He sighed. "And at last I'm here."

Home. Could he read my face? He was looking at me.

"Yes, home, my Anna, in spite of all I said." He gazed around him once again, and his eyes were tender.

"I've learned for myself, Father—" His words were soft, but he spoke them firmly. "There's nothing better out there to run away to. There wasn't much I saw that I liked—though at times it was hard to admit that."

He looked at me and I met his eyes gladly. "It really boils down to this: There's a price you pay for everything in life, Anna. I decided that Zion . . . the gospel . . . it's worth the price for me."

He put his arms around me. His wiry whiskers tickled the line of my cheek. "Welcome home, Petur," I whispered. "I'm so grateful we're all together, a family again."

Chapter Eighteen

I had no chance to see Owen until after the next evening's performance. I was very nervous. What kind of reception would greet me? I approached the small group of actors with caution, half wanting to slip on past them and hurry home. It was safe at home and Petur was waiting. It was not safe in this world—even here with Owen.

And perhaps even Owen would not understand about last night. I lingered on the fringe of the group while these doubts assailed me. The actors were happy and laughing, all flushed with their victory, caught up with one another in a world of their own making. I didn't really belong here . . .

I backed away. As if feeling my fears, Owen turned toward me. His eyes swept the cluster of faces and settled on mine. "Anna!" he called out loudly and motioned to me.

I couldn't just walk right up there beside him! I hesitated. A girl from the cast leaned close and said something that made him laugh. Oh, what was I doing here? I turned away quickly. But, hawklike, he caught my movement and swept down beside me.

"Anna, what happened last night? I missed you."

The stage group continued chattering, their world was intact still. Owen could move easily from world to world. This moment he belonged nowhere as much as beside me.

I told him. His eyes grew wide. "Well, bully for Petur! I knew he had the real stuff in him. I'm glad for you, Anna."

I smiled at him. He didn't know what his kindness meant to me.

"Are you still free to come with me tonight?"

I gulped, but nodded. Free to go *with him.* I hadn't portrayed it that way exactly. For some reason I'd covered it up, watered it down. There was to be a party with some of the young people after the drama. I had told my parents I was invited and wanted to go. That was all.

He took my hand. We walked back to the group together. It parted and let us in with no notice, no fuss. As long as I stood with my hand in Owen's I was part of them, not to be questioned or singled out. I knew that, and I was grateful. But deep inside me a little question teased and festered: What would they do—how would they accept me if I were alone, on my very own merits?

I stayed with the party much later than I had intended. Owen's company was an intoxication I found more and more difficult to resist. When at last we broke away he insisted on walking me all the way home. I consented. I was happy for the spare minutes with him.

We walked along slowly, not saying much, but at ease together. Ever since that rainy day on the mountain there had been something new and solid between us. He held my hand and began to sing softly, a tune with no words.

"What is that?"

"The song the Welsh girl sang while I played the harp."

It was haunting; it drew out my heart from me.

"What are the words in English?"

He sang them: "Conway is fair, Nevin is fair, the tips of the Mostyn trees are fair, the fairest place I ever know in the world is Meivod Valley."

I knew what the poet meant. I could close my eyes and sing with the same sure rhapsody of my island. "How does the rest go, Owen?"

"You want to hear more?"

"Oh, yes, sing it all for me."

"Bury me when I am dead"—his voice was uneven, ragged with tears and longing. How did he do that?—"in the trees under the oak leaves; you shall see a yellow-haired youth on my grave playing the harp."

He smiled at me, and without thinking I touched his thick brown hair with the tips of my fingers.

"There are two hearts in my bosom." His voice had dropped lower, aching with melancholy. "One is cold and the other warm; one is warm through love of her, and the other is cold through fear of losing her."

With the music still on his lips he moved closer and kissed my hair, then my cheek. His lips were so warm, so soft against my skin. I felt my flesh shudder with sensations I never had felt before.

He said nothing; we walked the last way in silence. At my door he squeezed my hand gently, then let it go. "Are you going to choir practice Saturday morning?"

"Oh, yes," I managed to whisper.

"I'll see you then."

He touched my fingers one last time, then turned and walked from me. I could scarcely catch my breath. The door opened behind me. Petur stood in the wedge of light that had brashly intruded into the quiet space of darkness belonging to me.

"Who is that boy?" He gazed after Owen. "Isn't . . . isn't he that Welsh kid who wouldn't fight me?"

I nodded.

"What are you doing out with him, Anna?"

"He walked me home. That's all."

I went into the house. I could feel Petur's disapproval in the gaze he turned on me. I ignored it. Perhaps it was all in my mind, borne of my own uncertainties. I hoped so. I certainly hoped so.

It was a new life, really, now that Petur was with us. He was a man grown, and a different person from the surly, emotional boy who had gone away. Petur and Haldora and the new house—each had worked a subtle change in the fabric of our family.

I often thought, watching Petur working with Father, or watching my mother as she sang to little Haldora and cradled her close, of how kind our Father in Heaven is to the patient. "God moves in mysterious ways"—I had seen that. He had worked a restoration in all our lives, and drawn blessings out of a darkness where we had seen nothing but suffering and despair.

The next Saturday morning I went to choir practice as usual, barely able to contain myself through the singing. Some impulse, some restless longing seized me. I felt I could not breathe in this closed-in space with the faces of all these ordinary people around me.

Once released I ran to the door. Would Owen be waiting? He was there. When he turned and saw me that smile lit his face and something within me sang. We walked off together through the streets and toward the low hills. We passed people, we tripped over people; I hardly noticed. I saw nothing, heard nothing but Owen.

The following day our family went to the Icelandic meeting. Of course, Petur was with us. In fact, he addressed the people and what he said left no doubt in anyone's mind as to Petur's standing. He may have digressed, he may have rebelled, but he had repented, he had gained a testimony for himself—something every Saint must do. He was accepted—forgiven and back in the fold. The young girl who watched him, with liquid brown eyes and a soft mouth, was a stranger to Spanish Fork. But she was Icelandic, newly come from a home with her aunt in Salt Lake. Sister Sveinsson, our dear Freyja Sveinsson, was her aunt also. The girl had no mother and father. She had come to live with the Sveinssons for a spell.

Petur walked her home when the meeting was over. Her little white hand rested on his arm. She knew him only as the handsome bearded young man, so strong and so tall, who had a touch of worldly fascination clinging to him, but a firm, sure testimony and a good new job. I watched them go off together. *Perhaps it is better*, I thought to myself. *The old Petur is dead. She will never be bothered by outgrown memories. There is nothing for her to see but the new man, who will always look grand in her eyes.*

I walked home with my parents and wondered what Owen was doing today. Did they sing Welsh songs where he went to church? I supposed not. I supposed the songs and the sermons were all in English. Other than that difference, surely, the two were the same—Latter-day Saints praying to the same God, holding the same priesthood, seeking the same salvation. Then why was I afraid? And what was I really afraid of? I didn't know.

Chapter Nineteen

On Wednesday evening I went to choir practice and forced myself to sing till the songs moved inside me and absorbed my concentration. We were late getting out. I couldn't find Owen anywhere. He had promised to be there. I was confused. It was not like Owen to fail me. A crisp wind blew down from the canyons. After waiting some minutes I pulled my shawl tight against the wind and walked home. Perhaps something had happened to prevent him. I knew that could be—I who had failed to show up the night Petur came home, with no censure from Owen. I tried to tell myself these things, but the coldness inside me was more horrible than the wind.

Petur *had* changed. He seemed purposeful and forceful in all he did. There were no swinging extremes of thought or emotion. He seemed to have come to grips with himself and what he wanted out of a world he admitted to be imperfect—but which he accepted, along with its imperfections.

Twice during the week he spent time with the girl from Iceland. Gudrun Olafsson was her name. She seemed a sweet thing. A little shy, and more than happy to follow his lead. *Just the kind of girl*, I thought, *to complement this new Petur.*

Myself, I lived for Saturday morning. I did my hair that morning with special care, and dressed in a skirt about which

Owen had once complimented me. How could I sit through the hours before I would see him? How could I sing with my heart in my throat?

When the practice was over I walked cautiously to the door—suddenly afraid, beset with uncertainty. I looked around me. At first I saw nothing. I moved outside. I straightened the hem on my dress and fussed with my gloves, stealing glances here and there. I could not see Owen. I drew a deep breath to steady my heart. What should I do now? Should I walk up the mountain pathway alone? Perhaps for some reason he was there, waiting. How obvious that would appear! I hesitated. Yet I knew I would go up there.

Never before had the walk seemed so long, so filled with small irritations, so unlovely. My mind drew half a dozen different scenes as they might transpire when I topped the ridge and saw him. I resisted them all. I also resisted the cruel little voice that kept saying: *He will not be on the mountain. You will not find him.*

And what then? I didn't face that question either.

When I stood on the crest of the hill and found it barren, when my eyes scanned the empty expanse until tears blurred their gaze, there was nothing but a confusion of pain inside me. I could not hate Owen; I could not be angry. I only felt tired. Tired and strangely empty. I walked on home. When I arrived there, exhausted and wilted, Petur looked me up and down.

"Choir practice is over at ten. Where have you been, Anna?"

I could not believe my ears! I looked sharply at him. "Mother and Father put together are not as picky as you."

"I'm merely curious, Anna."

I didn't believe him. "I answer to them, Petur. Surely, that's enough." I pushed past him, blinking hard to keep the tears from my eyes.

It was a long, lonely day for me. I had nothing to savor, nothing to think about, nothing I dared look forward to. I tried to keep busy, but work was a lame substitute for what I was missing.

At last the day wound into evening. We ate a light supper, a Saturday night supper—simple fare. I pulled out the old tin tub to bathe the children. Haldora was fussy and ready for bed. We would bathe her first and tuck her away. I had moved on to Sina, up to my elbows in soap and water, when I heard voices. Men's voices and friendly laughter. I strained to listen. Perhaps it was Petur come back with some of his friends, perhaps callers for Father. I leaned back over the tub to rinse Sina's hair. She shoved her fists into her eyes and screwed her face up. "You're worse than the baby," I scolded gently.

"Well, at least you do it quickly. Mother doesn't. She takes twice as long and gets all of the soap in my eyes."

I kissed her on the soapy forehead. "I'll try to hurry."

"Please do," Mother said from the doorway. "There's a visitor here you might like to see."

I was curious; I was more than curious. I toweled Sina's hair down, wiped my own soaked hands, and peeked cautiously around the corner.

Father was on his knees by the fireplace. Kneeling beside him, explaining the fine points of a strip of wood carving, was *Owen.* Owen—the grin on his face, his voice warm to his subject. Owen kneeling beside my father in my own home!

My fingers clutched at my throat. I backed away from the doorway. He mustn't see me like this! What was he doing here? What madness had possessed him?

My mother was watching. "I'll finish Sina and do Gesli, Anna. You go on out there."

I didn't want her to know how much it mattered. I straightened my hair with uncertain fingers and took off my apron, pulled down my sleeves that were still limp and damp. Owen's voice rang out in a laugh; my father's answered. To think of hearing Owen's voice—of seeing him here!

I moved slowly into the room. Neither one had seen me. There was a comradeship between them that I could feel. I leaned against Mother's long table and drew my breath in. Owen turned; his eyes found my face. The happiness in them compensated me for the long, wretched hours I had just lived through.

"Anna. Hello, there." He grinned. "Remember last summer when you told me your father worked with wood and might enjoy seeing some of my designs?" He cocked his round head. It hadn't been quite like that. I nodded and tried to smile back. My father looked at me. Carefully.

"This young man is quite gifted," he said.

I tried to hide the joy his words stirred. "Do you think so, Father? He's made a harp—his own harp, with such carvings on it!"

"You've seen this harp?"

I swallowed. My insides were trembling. Why did he ask the question that way? "Not close up, Father. I've actually seen it only once—at the same time you did—when he played in Provo on Pioneer Day. Don't you remember?"

My father sat back on his heels and thought for a moment. "I do remember; I remember the music. I remember the dancing—" He looked at Owen. "So you've fashioned a harp. That's a little more demanding than fancy woodworking, I'd be thinking."

The tension I could read in the lines of Owen's face relaxed a little. So even he wasn't thoroughly sure of himself here! Or perhaps he had just been concerned that I would ruin things for him—for us. That was probably it, more likely.

"There's a spirit in such work, for certain." A soft expression played over his face. "Even the wood used to form the harp has a sort of spirit, a wholeness—a life force one must respect—"

"I know what you mean, son. You must invite the spirit of music into the wood, in through *your* hands and heart—a heart in tune with the ancient secrets."

Owen looked at my father. His eyes were moist and deep. "How do you understand, sir?"

"I have fashioned things with the spirit also."

After that even Owen forgot my existence. They sketched designs for one another and created a pattern to fit around our mantel. A glowing was on them. Owen had brought a tool to show my father that he had never seen. It had to be demonstrated and tried over and over, experimented with and admired. The hour was late when at last Owen rose with a sigh.

"I've imposed, Brother Jonsson. I had no intention of staying so long."

"Where is imposition?" My father was truly offended. "You and I, son, together, have created beauty with our hands and our hearts. That's a rare thing, Owen."

Impulsively Owen reached out for my father's hand and hugged it more than he shook it. I had to do something! I walked boldly to the door, and then through it with him, tensed for a word of reprimand to stay me. But no word came. We stood in the darkness together. He reached for my hand.

"What a father you have, Anna!"

He was pressing something against my palm: a limp piece of paper. I closed my fingers around it.

"That's why I came," he went on in a whisper. "The note will explain it. I'm sorry, Anna. I'm so sorry about last week and this morning." His fingers found my hair. Those magic fingers, running like silver though my tangled locks. "How I've missed you, Anna!"

The door was still ajar. With my foot against it I pushed gently. The slice of light narrowed. Owen stepped closer. His lips found the curve of my cheek and rested there gently while his arms drew me in till his warmth was my warmth, his breath my breath, his heartbeat my heartbeat.

With reluctance I drew away. "You must go now." I expected the door to burst open upon us at any moment.

"I know that. Read the note quickly, but carefully." His warm lips found my forehead. "Sweet dreams, my Anna."

He was gone. *My Anna* . . . I breathed, with his voice still upon me, and the feel of his lips in the darkness. Elder Thorderson had said that, but it hadn't meant what it meant now. The difference was too all-consuming, too grand to ignore.

I would need to go back inside. Somehow. I slid, a shadow, around the door. If I closed it softly, whisper-soft . . .

"You'll catch a cold, Anna. Come quickly inside."

Sane and normal, my mother's voice. But the magic lingered. The magic was still in this room. I looked past my father, and tried to hurry past him as well. But he would not have it.

"That's a very nice boy there," he said, "but he always has been. From the beginning, isn't that right?"

I nodded my head. I don't think I could have spoken. I was very grateful that my mother had turned the lamp low and snuffed out the candles. "Character will surface, one way or another. I've seen it happen time after time. And the lad is gifted." He chuckled softly. "He's taught me a thing or two."

"Good night, Father," I said, slipping softly by him. Anything more I tried to say would reveal myself.

"Good night, daughter. It's been a pleasant evening, thanks to you."

What did he mean, saying "thanks to you"? It was I who knew Owen, whose friendship had brought him here. It could simply be that, but I didn't think so. There had been something more in my father's voice when he said the words.

Chapter Twenty

Petur was getting married. I had seen it coming—anyone with two eyes in his head had. When he was with Gudrun Saturday night he asked her. And, of course, the girl consented. On Sunday morning he spoke officially to Brother Sveinsson asking her hand. Brother Sveinsson was happy to give his consent and the matter was settled.

I had saved Owen's letter until early Sunday morning. I had little choice. If I had lit a candle to read, Mother would have come scolding and discovered the secret missive. It was torture to wait. But I closed my eyes and relived those moments with Owen beside me and fell asleep with the feel of his lips on my skin.

Alone on my hill the next morning I unfolded the paper, hungry, yet apprehensive. I read it through. Then I read it through again. There was much to digest here; some shadow, some light. Owen's words read:

> Dear Anna, I am so sorry I was not there to meet you. We've run into a bit of a snag. Do you remember seeing Brother Morgan when we were walking Saturday morning? He told my parents he had "caught" us together. Not only that. He had seen us more than one time—I believe he's been purposefully spying. Can you imagine that of a grown man? I'm disgusted. My mother got angry and my father went white—he always does that when something upsets my mother.

She *got angry* at the thought of her son seeing me? Something inside me turned hard and hot.

> I have been forbidden—what an ugly word—to see you, Anna. I must be careful, at least for a while, till I figure this through. Upsetting my parents further won't help us any. I am coming to your house with this letter. I don't know what will happen . . .

I smiled, remembering.

> but I must see you. Could you meet me at the old Stoddard cabin, Monday night right after dark? I hope so. I will look forward till then. Please forgive me, Anna.

"Sincerely, Owen. With love, Owen." Perhaps he had scratched both out. There were several blotches. At the bottom he had written, "Yours, Owen." I traced the words, as I had traced the print of his lips on my cheek.

I would not cry like a baby. I would not! I walked back and got ready for church with the others. The news of the day, of course, was Petur's engagement. Everyone hugging and shaking hands, the old ladies crying, even a young girl or two sniffling into her handkerchief.

I would have lived through it; I would have made it except for Petur. What an old meddler he had become! And malicious, too. After lingering, as the whole family had to, for best wishes and congratulations, I was more than anxious to get away. Petur came up beside me, his arm around Gudrun's waist. Gudrun simpered at me. I ignored her as best I could.

"Now, Anna, there's joy enough of this kind to go around." Petur smiled down upon me and little Gudrun shadowed his smile. "I've asked Gunner Christenson over for dinner. Gudrun will be there—"

I was seething inside. "Does Mother know this?"

"Oh, yes, Mother approves entirely." He took a step closer, bent toward me, and lowered his voice. "You know, Anna, Gunner is very interested in you. You need to be kinder—kinder, is all I ask." I glared at him with all the strength of the storm inside me. He glared right back, and his voice took on an edge. "You be careful, Anna. I know all about last night—"

You know all about nothing!

"The Welsh boy has no business coming to see you. Take care, little Anna. Your whole future is at stake."

I turned my back on him. It was the only thing I could do, except cry out loud. I walked home alone, as fast as I could. No one tried to stop me. The tears blinded my eyes and splashed down my cheeks. They washed away Owen's kiss. I could no longer feel it. I could no longer see the pleasure in Owen's eyes. I could only see Petur's face and hear the ugly words echoing: "Your whole future is at stake. You be careful, Anna. The Welsh boy had no business—"

I choked on the rage that welled up with fires of anguish inside my being.

Somehow I made it through that day. Gunner came to dinner. Gudrun sat beside Petur and Gunner by me. Petur was in his glory; he spared me nothing. I gave him stare for stare, word for word, pride for pride; he would never break me, never see into my crying heart.

Poor Gunner; he knew nothing of this. He was pleasant with me, and pleased—so obviously pleased with the occasion. It was not fair to this pleasant boy to be building his hopes up. He was Icelandic. Did that make all the difference? I had trusted Petur. Was there no one to understand?

By the time Monday night came I was in a fever of anticipation. I had planned my excuse and I thought it a good one: I would take some apples to Sister Palsson and then drop by Brother Johnson's house to borrow a book from his library. He loaned his Icelandic books to our people on a regular basis. I could actually do both things quickly and not lie at all, and then tell Mother I went for a walk after. Or I could skip the book and give myself more time.

It was a simple plan and it would have worked perfectly for me. But at the last minute—the very last minute, when my hair was all combed, the apples packed in a basket, my hand on my shawl—little Gesli started begging to come along with me.

I felt panic rise inside me. I hushed him away. But he was stubborn in his resolve. My mother considered. I protested, but that tipped the scales against me.

"Let the boy go. You could use the company, Anna. Gesli goes nowhere; the walk would be good for him."

I was very close to tears. I could think of nothing to save the situation. Samuel came up beside me. "Is it all right if I come, too?"

I looked at him sharply. There was something about his voice. He winked at me as he reached for his cap. What could he be up to?

"Yes, yes, I'd like you to come." I had nothing to lose.

"Let's go." He grabbed Gesli's hand. Poor Gesli. He really was thrilled to be coming along. Samuel talked with him, showed him things of interest, enticed him—enticed him off the path, got him caught up in exploring some scent Samuel started him on.

As soon as he disappeared out of sight, Samuel said very softly, "We'll hurry to Sister Palsson's with you. Then you can go off—on your own—I'll take care of Gesli. There's a new duck blind down by the river he'd like me to show him. He'll be so excited he'll forget all about you."

I stared at Samuel. He smiled rather shyly. "It's all right, Anna. I know you—well, I know you have things to do. It's all right by me."

What was he saying?

"I'll remind Mother how much you like browsing through books—that's nothing but the truth. If that doesn't do it, I'll put the idea in her mind of how you love to take walks, and it is a beautiful evening—"

I hugged him quickly. I couldn't help myself. "Samuel, do you know—"

"I don't know anything, Anna." He cocked his head. "Let's keep it that way."

Dear Samuel! Gesli came back and we skipped to the Palssons', then raced each other the last few yards. Samuel ran the basket of apples inside for me, to avoid the possibility of a long conversation with Sister Palsson. It took only a minute or two. At the bridge we parted. I walked in the direction of Brother Johnson's, then doubled back and turned down the lane that led out to the Stoddard homestead and the old burned-out cabin set back from the road.

I saw at once that there was a faint light inside the cabin. My heart quickened. I peeked through the charred window hole. Owen sat on the floor, a piece of paper spread over his knee. He was scribbling intently. When he looked up and saw me he slipped the paper inside his jacket and smiled. But not his wide, boyish grin. There was something of pain in his smile. But his eyes were all gladness. He came around and pulled me inside.

"It's been so long, Anna. Why does it seem so long since I've seen you?"

The touch of his hand, warm and sure, sent a current of pleasure through me. "It wasn't easy tonight," I said. "Will it always be like this?"

His brow wrinkled into lines of concern. I loved that expression even more than his comical grin.

"I told you."

"You told me what?" he echoed.

"I told you you'd get in trouble for being seen with an Icelandic girl."

"Well, it's ridiculous," he protested. "I still can't believe it. It makes no sense."

"Very little of what people do makes sense, Owen."

The grin came then. Brief, and in spite of himself.

"Does this mean I won't ever see you?"

"No, Anna. Of all the things it may mean, I won't let it mean that."

"You used to tell me it doesn't matter what people think." My voice sounded angry. "Have you changed your mind?"

"Not a bit. I don't care about people—public opinion, or whatever they call it. It's just—my parents. I don't know what to do about them."

A hot fear shot through me. "Why don't they like me? Is it just—" I couldn't make myself finish.

"It's not you—they don't even know you, Anna. It's fear on their part more than prejudice, I think. They just need a little time."

I was shaking my head. "A little time won't make any difference with them. Even a lot of time won't. And meanwhile, what about us?"

He took a step back and looked me over. His eyes held mischief. "Us, Anna? What concern is this? I thought you disdained me. The obnoxious Welsh boy—"

I stomped my foot at him. He grabbed for my hand and drew me closer.

"I'm sorry, Anna." The words came out breathless and gentle. He kept hold of my hand, weaving his fingers around my fingers. "Anna . . . have you ever loved anyone before?"

I considered carefully. "Once, Owen." I thought of my beloved Elder Thorderson. "Once . . . in a way." But it had not been like this. I could see that now.

"I've never felt anything special for a girl before you, Anna. And with you I knew right from the start—from the first time I saw you."

I felt a shudder of what must be joy sweep over my frame.

"Could you skip choir Wednesday nights and meet me instead?"

It was tempting. "It wouldn't work," I told him. "Mother always asks, 'How was practice this evening?' And what of the others missing me and saying something?"

"Of course. You're right." He pushed his brown hair back with his fingers. "What about Thursdays? Could you meet me above the bench Thursday night?"

My throat had gone dry. I swallowed to ease it. "I always go out by myself on long walks . . . no one ought to suspect me. But what of yourself?"

"Don't you worry about me; I'll be there. This Thursday then?"

I nodded. Only three more days till I would see him again.

He let go of my hand. "Don't worry, Anna." He brushed his lips across my forehead. My knees went weak. I longed for him to hold me. I walked to the door—or what used to be the door. There were only some boards there, a few boards nailed across the entrance. A clump of sage squatted tenaciously right in the middle. I stepped across it.

"I'll go first?" His eyes were so warm when they watched me.

"Yes, I've work to do." He patted his pocket. What was it he had been writing? I waved to him, like a schoolgirl. He kissed his hand—it looked gallant the way he did it, not silly. He watched after me for a moment. I felt his eyes. It may seem strange, but I felt his love reach out with his gaze and it rested upon me, more soft than the evening shadows that attended me home.

Chapter Twenty-One

Plans went forward for Petur's wedding. I helped my mother and Freyja with details of sewing and cooking, but my heart wasn't in it. My mother seemed quietly happy. She had her baby—soft, lovable little Haldora. And now a wedding—security, promise of more babies to come.

My father. Well, life had returned to my father. He was himself again and more, if that could be. A dimension of understanding, a new patience and awareness rested upon him: *knowledge of self.* I think it came back to that. I suppose if we struggle to be receptive, life has countless ways to increase that perilous, precious knowledge. Some men shun it altogether. But never my father. And this experience with Petur had taught him much, had strengthened something which was already good and rare inside him.

Petur had come home reformed, reconverted. I knew that. He had also become a fanatic of sorts. He did everything by the book. There was no room for error, for question, for the least diversion. So where did that leave me? In the gray field of nonadherence. I knew that. Disapproved of, perhaps even despaired of, if all were known.

It was I who despaired! Petur's course was a safe one; safe and direct. I had lost Petur. He had his path to pursue, but I had mine. And the two seemed in no way compatible with one another.

I met Owen that Thursday night and the following Thursday. And we discovered another problem: The days had turned cold. In the evenings on the heights a cold wind would be blowing. It was not feasible to stay long in that wind. Was the extent of our meetings to be a wretched ten minutes, shouting endearments for the wind to snatch from our hearing, perched on a slab of cold stone rubbing chilled hands together?

Friday morning I walked down to the schoolhouse to deliver my lessons. I stopped on the way to buy thread at the store for my mother. I was drawn by the cheerful warmth of the place and I browsed a little. The chatter of the two women in front of me blended in with the rest, until all at once I recognized a name from out of the midst of their speaking, and that name hurled their words at me with a sudden force.

"Well, you know my Owen. He was always one to go his own way. He's a stubborn boy."

"But a good boy, Marged—you know that. I'm sure he'll come to his senses if given some time."

Sister Davies had nearly the same name as my mother! I had forgotten that. She didn't seem to agree with her friend. "His father has already tried to lure him with gifts of land," she complained, "if he'll marry young Angharad. She's a pretty, sweet little thing and he's always liked her—"

I flattened myself in among the sacks of potatoes and onions, a small bent shape with my back to the women.

"I don't understand the lad."

Bless the other woman. She laughed heartily. "Well, Marged, now, if you did, you'd be the rare one indeed and could set up practice advising the rest of us poor, struggling mothers."

The voices grew faint. The two ladies stood at the counter, their backs to me. I didn't catch Sister Davies's reply, but I didn't need to. I had heard enough—I had heard too much as it was.

I walked to the school in a sort of stupor. My mind was angry and my feelings bruised, and the two could not function together. Miss Fletcher knew something was wrong; I was scarcely coherent. At last she looked up from her book.

"Come, Anna. You must tell me what it is. Perhaps I can help you."

"No, no," I replied in alarm, "even you could not help me."

She smiled in a strange, secret way. "Anna, later this evening I will be here at the schoolhouse correcting notebooks and preparing my lessons. Owen Davies walks past the schoolhouse every Friday at just seven o'clock." She raised an eyebrow. "Why don't you come back then when I've had some time to review your work?"

I tried to thank her, but she waved me aside. I stumbled home, feeling much as I had when I'd been a schoolgirl: miserable and uncertain and unaccepted.

It was easy to leave the house on Miss Fletcher's instructions: A teacher's requests are regarded as next to sacred. He was there when I walked in the building. She must have warned him. He looked anxiously into my face. Miss Fletcher brushed past us.

"I've less work than I thought, my dears. It seems I'm all finished. Put out the lights when you leave. Lock the doors, Owen." She handed him her key. "Will you return this to me before you go home? And, oh, Anna, would Tuesday night be all right to review your lessons? Same time, dear."

She didn't wait for response from me. Owen took my cold hands and rubbed them between his own.

"What's the matter, Anna?"

I told him. He listened, beetle-browed. When I had finished he remained silent for a moment or two. I could see his mind working, struggling behind the fine, troubled eyes.

"Anna . . ." His voice was so soft I could barely hear it. "Would you try to understand her . . . a little . . . please?"

This was not what I had expected to hear. I had no reply ready.

"In many ways she's like you, Anna. She feels about Wales much the way you feel about Iceland. She hangs on—she clings to her fears—"

I turned angrily from him. I wanted sympathy, not this distasteful challenge.

"Well, Anna, we must come to grips with this somehow. She's not ready to understand us, but surely you—"

"Why surely me? Why *always* me, Owen?"

He ignored my ridiculous question. "I love her, Anna. I understand some of the reasons behind how she acts; I don't want to hurt her . . ."

His voice was so terribly tender. It pierced right through me.

"I should hate to force you to hurt your mother, Owen. That answers many of the questions we've struggled with, don't you think? Perhaps you ought to simply marry the sweet, pretty Welsh girl, what's-her-name!"

"You talk nonsense, Anna. You always talk nonsense when you're upset."

I was fighting my tears, determined that he should not see me cry. "Then I'd better stop talking and spare you this loathsome nonsense."

I ran for the door, pulling my coat on over my shoulders. By now I was crying. He hesitated too long. By the time he followed I was lost somewhere in the darkness. He let me go. How long he sat in the schoolhouse in misery I have no way of knowing. If he was half as unhappy as I, I don't know how he bore it. I moved through the weekend by force of habit, like one in a trance. I could eat nothing. I tossed in my sleep; I suffered nightmares. The Sabbath became a torture to grit my teeth and live through somehow.

For the third time since Petur's engagement Gunner came to dinner. He was gaining confidence—in other words, growing yet more obnoxious to me. Petur grinned like a cat that had swallowed a bird; he enjoyed my discomfort. I could almost have hated him then if I had let myself.

Petur's wedding was set for late spring. They would live in the dugout until he could build Gudrun a proper house. He was very happy. I didn't mind seeing Petur happy; if he had just been less smug! Wasn't that always Petur's way, everything or nothing. Hot or cold. Right or wrong.

When would I see Owen again? Would he come on Thursday? Oh, how awkward it would be!

Tuesday evening I walked to the schoolhouse. Miss Fletcher would have something for me to take my mind off myself: comments and criticism, new lessons to prepare, some exciting challenge. I looked forward to it.

It was warm inside the schoolhouse and as cozy as home. I took my coat off and hung it on one of the wall pegs. Miss Fletcher wasn't sitting at her desk waiting for me. Owen Davies was. He blinked when he saw me enter and his eyes showed his pleasure. But his face remained cautious and closed.

He rose and walked to me.

"If this keeps up I'll never get anywhere with my studies. How did you bribe Miss Fletcher?"

"It didn't take much." That smile, that irrepressible grin! I began to tremble.

"Thank heaven for this," he said fiercely, "otherwise I'd have gone mad."

This—our warm, lit haven and Miss Fletcher's contrivance.

"Sit down, Anna, please. I have something for you."

How warm he could make me feel! With some ceremony he seated me on a chair at the front of the room. Then he made me close my eyes. I could feel him moving, hear something rustling.

"Hold out your hands," he instructed.

I cupped my hands in the air in front of me. Something touched them, something hard and smooth to the touch. I ran my finger across it. There were carvings of some kind and a gentle curving. I opened my eyes.

In my hands I held a carved wooden spoon, the fine grain polished so that a dozen shades rose and swelled and diminished along its surface. It was the most exquisite thing I had ever seen. I smoothed my finger along the dished edge.

"You made this, Owen?"

"They call it a 'love spoon' in Wales. All the young men make one when they become serious in the matter of romance."

I thrilled to his words, but attempted to hide my emotion. "Do they always carve them this way—this well?"

"The carvings are very much a personal matter. Some designs —love knots and roses and such—become universal. For those lacking imagination and skill."

There was a touch of pride in his voice, he could not hide it.

"But these carvings—" My voice held my awe like the sea holds the sun, like the rain barrel holds the pure dews from heaven.

"They're designs that mean something to me—and to you."

"The seagull." I traced his shape, one wing extended outward from the spoon in a graceful arc.

"The seagull—of course, he is Iceland, mainly. See the wave and the rock he soars above?"

I nodded, a sweet ache in my throat. He continued.

"But the seagull is also Salt Lake, Anna, and the way you felt when you came here—and the rock he flies over is also your mountain and the spot where we meet and talk."

I nodded again. I touched the book twined with sego lilies. "I like this," I whispered.

"The book is Icelandic poetry hopelessly tangled with desert flowers—beauty stranded out here in the desert." He touched my hand, tracing his finger over my skin as I had traced his carvings.

"And the harp?" I breathed.

"The harp is music. The music of your heart and mine as they blend together. The harmony of our love, the majesty, Anna . . ."

He could barely speak the words. I could feel his trembling. He leaned forward and covered my lips with his, claimed them with sweet insistence.

"The harp is also a promise," he murmured against my mouth. "I love you, Anna. I shall fill all your days with the music of my love."

Tears trailed down my cheeks. I could not stop them. I could barely breathe for the pain of this joy.

"*I love you, I love you!*" I cried the words from the depth of my soul, and his soul responded, and the music of heaven moved through us.

We drew apart. I had to say it, I at least had to try. "For centuries, Owen, the young men of Wales have carved love spoons?"

He nodded. "For nearly three hundred years."

"But never one like this, with such skill and such spirit, such sensitivity to the soul of the woman he loves."

He was moved. But I meant every word, and he knew it.

"It is my attempt at poetry. I'm not like you, Anna." He spoke the words with a simple humility. "You *are* poetry, Anna. Your voice, the words you speak, the way you move—"

I cried out, but he stopped my protests with kisses till I drew back breathless again.

"I must let you go. Somehow." He wound his strong fingers into my hair, like the tendrils of desert lilies. He held me closer, resting safely within his arms.

The door flew open with the sound of the waves on the rock, with the anger of thunder.

Samuel stood in the doorway. His breathing was ragged. His eyes were wild with the storm of his coming.

"Quick, Anna. Petur is on his way here. He's close behind."

I felt panic race through my body. "Why? How—"

"I'm not certain. I think he only suspects. If he doesn't find you—"

I moved nervously toward the door. Was my coat on the peg still? Did I hang it there years ago? Samuel brought it for me. I struggled my arms inside, my hot fingers still clasping the solid coolness of the spoon. Owen stood there watching.

"He must not find us," I pleaded, anxious to stir him.

"We are past the time of running. Let him find us, Anna."

"Oh, no!" Fear froze the currents of panic to solid pain. "You don't understand. You can't bend Petur, you can't touch him—your mother and father are nothing compared to him—" I could hear myself begging. I hated the sound in my ears.

"Do you want to run away, Anna?"

"Yes!" I said fiercely.

"You are a woman; you are his sister." His voice was still gentle. "I am a man. I cannot slink away from him into the darkness—like an animal—like a craven—"

His eyes were clear and unafraid, his voice was steady. "Then I'll stay with you," I said. I walked over to Samuel and kissed him. "God bless you, my darling. Can you slip away safely again?"

"Don't worry." He glanced once at Owen, then turned. "I'll see you at home."

I shut the door behind him. I took my coat off and hung it back on the peg. I sat down beside Owen and waited for the real storm to blow in from the night.

Chapter Twenty-Two

He came. He burst through the door, sure he would surprise us. We sat calmly; we held him with calm eyes.

He blustered a bit till he got his bearings. "What are you doing here, Anna?" It was a demand, not a question he asked.

"I am talking with Owen."

"You met him here on purpose!" Such accusation in his voice. I would have smiled if I had dared. "And this isn't the first time. You've been meeting him secretly, haven't you?"

"I won't deny it. But it is nothing to bring you out into the night."

Petur's eyes grew wide. "I cannot believe this of you, Anna. How wicked, how foolish."

"It's neither, Petur. I have done nothing to be ashamed of."

"You've lost your senses. You're throwing your life away on this . . . this . . ."

"Welshman," I offered. "What an awful, awful word."

"Don't be smart with me, Anna. You don't know what's for your best good, girl; it's plain to see that."

I stood without even knowing and faced him squarely. "You've lived your own life from the start. No one has stood in your way. You've hurt people, you've made mistakes. This is my life, Petur. I have the same rights as you."

I thought Owen would cheer; I could feel his pleasure beside me. My words stopped Petur. He glared at me with bristling eyes.

"There's no reasoning with you. Two wrongs don't make a right. I know better, Anna. I know better than you do what's right for—"

"What's right for *me*?" I didn't mean to shout the words, but I must have. He bent backward as if from a blow.

"Come home with me, Anna. Right now."

For the first time he looked at Owen. The steady blue eyes met his like a wall he was about to run into. He withdrew with startled haste. He ignored the danger and reached for me with a long arm. Owen stood between us, a sudden slender shield. For the first time he spoke.

"It is enough. You have made your point, Petur. I will see your sister safely home. You can go now."

If it was ever to come to blows, the moment was now. Owen was magnificent, and we had the advantage. From the start surprise was on our side. But I held my breath still. There was a moment or two when I wondered.

"All right, have it your way. It's not worth any more trouble to me." He turned away. But it must have been hard to walk off feeling so defeated. At the door he hurled one last shot. "I said 'have it your way.' But it will be for the very last time. I assure you of that."

He left, but the room was still thick with his presence. His threat pounded in my ears. "He means it, Owen."

"Of course he means it, Anna."

"Well, I'm afraid."

"Don't, don't be afraid. Fear won't help you, Anna. Fear is master, never servant—you must know that. Try . . . try to understand."

"That won't help either."

"But it will. You and I—we're going to be okay, Anna. Understanding will pave the way. Without it we might shrivel up with bitterness and be useless to each other. Here—come, sit beside me."

He drew my chair very close to his. We sat touching each other with his arm around my shoulder. "I'll tell you a story. This is a story about a young Welsh girl. A pretty girl—as most Welsh girls are." He laughed. "Smile with me, Anna. She didn't know that the prettiest girls were stuck off in Iceland." I shook my head at him and smiled. I could not resist him.

"The young Welsh girl married her childhood sweetheart, a village boy. His father was the local butcher and the son worked with him, and the young couple knew some prosperity. Two sons came to bless their home, then a beautiful daughter. But then hard times struck. Sickness swept through the village. And it did not spare the young family. When it was through, the old father was claimed by the sickness, and so was the daughter, the baby daughter that died in her mother's arms.

"There was no food, no money. The young father had been sick unto death himself and he could not work. They lost their home, their business. They left the village with dozens of other families, looking for work. The girl had one thing to cling to: her little sister went with them—to help, for the young wife was pregnant again, and to comfort, for she could not accept the loss of her baby."

"I don't like this story," I said.

"Will you hear it, my Anna?"

"For you."

He smiled with his eyes. "They came to a village where holes had been dug in the ground, blind black tunnels that could swallow men's souls. It was here they settled. For the tunnels meant work and money and food. Merthyr Tydfil, a village named after a princess, a village of steel where the first locomotive to draw a train along rails came into existence. Merthyr Tydfil, the village where I was born."

"You were the third son." I wished I could help him. "Were there any more daughters?"

"Three. And each one born dead." I shuddered. "The Welsh mother began to lose hope; she began to grow tired. Her two sons went into the pit with their father. There was nothing beyond daily existence to live for. That and the little sister who was her comfort."

I felt it. I felt his words.

"Then a miracle happened. A simple, quiet miracle. You know it—"

"The Mormon missionaries?"

He nodded. "Their lives changed. They had something to live for at last, something to work for—something to hope for." His eyes took on pleasure. I drew a long breath of relief.

"The Welsh woman was happy. She possessed more than she ever had dreamed life could hold. But her husband desired to emigrate to Zion—leave the homeland for some far, unknown destination. It frightened her timid heart. This was home to her. She was happy, content with their lot. He persisted. There were no black pits in Zion. A man could buy land there. A man could breathe good clean air and work under the sun—not under tons of pressed earth.

"She consented. She saw what it would mean for him. And her little sister was more excited at the prospect of going than anyone else. She was in a fever to get to Zion! This precious sister was more like a child, like the daughters she'd lost. If Bronwyn wanted to go—how could Marged deny her?

"They saved and sacrificed for long months. When at last the time came they booked passage on a ship. The young sister, Bronwyn, was terrified of water. For the first few days she wouldn't even come out of the hold, much less go near the railing. She tried to laugh her fears away and her sister helped her, and it seemed things would go well for them all." Owen sighed.

"But they didn't. They never do in real life, do they?"

"It can seem that way." Owen's eyes were deep and sad. "There was much sickness on board the ship. Bronwyn caught whatever it was and became very ill. Marged nursed her until she herself was exhausted. She left the care of her own children to other women, living exclusively for her sister. When Bronwyn died it nearly broke her heart. And perhaps the worst of it was the dead girl's fear of the water. Near the end she had pleaded, 'Don't let them put me down into the ocean!' She begged her sister, over and over again, until Marged was nearly mad—"

"Don't, Owen," I pleaded myself, "I can't bear to hear it." I didn't realize that I was crying. He wiped my eyes.

"Of course in the end there was nothing else—they had to do it . . ."

"They buried her in the ocean. Your poor little mother . . ." I nestled my head into the warmth of his neck. "Thank you, Owen. Thank you for telling me. Has your mother had any more daughters?"

"One more born dead. Three months early."

I shuddered. I thought about little Dena and the pain was new, as though I felt it for the very first time. I thought of Haldora and the needs of a mother's love.

"I'll walk you home now. Only because I know I must."

I clung to his hand the entire way up to my house. My heart, my whole being were singing with love for Owen.

"Shall I take you inside? Would that be better?"

"No, I'd best go alone. But I will see you tomorrow night?" We made arrangements. I knew I would need him. I slipped my hand that still clung to the love spoon inside my pocket. I could conceal it there with ease.

Just my father was waiting, sitting quietly in his chair. I walked cautiously in and sunk down on the stool beside him.

"Is Mother in bed?"

"An hour since. You're out late, Anna." There was no censure in his voice.

"Have you spoken with Petur?"

"Oh, yes. Would you like to have your say?"

I felt tongue-tied. Where to begin and how to express it. "I love him, Father." It was the worst thing I could have said.

"What, the Welsh boy?"

"The Welsh boy! His name is Owen. He's a person like any other, a Latter-day Saint."

"And you think you love him?"

"I didn't say that, Father."

"All right, all right." He closed the book that lay in his lap. "I don't know, Anna. It's hard to advise another person, even someone you love. But from all I know of you—" He opened his hands up as though helpless to do less than he was doing. "You're so Icelandic. Marriage is hard, even when there is much in common. You may think—" He caught himself. "You may really love him. But living together is a different matter—"

I started to protest. "No, hear me out. You are young, you are both very young. The best I can tell you—in all conscience, daughter—is to wait awhile, give this affection some time, and meanwhile see other young men—"

"You mean other Icelanders." I stood up on shaky feet. There was no help here. *No help here.* I was swimming in pain.

"I'm tired, Father. Can we talk about this tomorrow?"

He didn't reply. He watched me walk out of the room. Perhaps he, too, felt it, and knew something was different between us that neither of us could help.

The next day life went on as though nothing had happened. Petur glared at me, to be sure, but was that something new? At first I felt a sense of relief; I abhor confrontations. But as the day progressed I recognized the truth and faced it. They would treat this whole thing as a trifle, an unpleasant flare-up that, fortunately, had passed over and blown itself out. Perhaps Anna would take the advice of her father. Perhaps constant contact with Gunner would change her mind. And there was Petur's wedding to set before her, the perfect example of a young person choosing wisely and well.

I felt sick inside. Helping Mother care for Haldora, making pies together, there was no word spoken of me and Owen. They chose to ignore it, to hope against hope it would go away.

I told Owen so that night and watched his eyes squint into their worried line.

"Waiting will not change them. Not one of them one bit. Will it change you, Anna? Change how you feel about me?"

I shook my head.

"Come with me, then." He took my hand. "Pull your scarf up tightly. The wind has a bite to it, Anna."

We walked up the hill together. The wind was behind us. It pushed us forward with friendly gusts. At the top we stood breathless, looking down upon the houses, the fields beyond, the wider expanse of sky and the far ring of mountains—always the distant mountains to draw the eye and pull the spirit past the body's frail limits. We felt it today: the scope and the majesty.

"That's our world, Anna, yours and mine. It may not be perfect. But it will do, it will do well for us, I believe."

He turned me to face him. His hands were warm still in spite of the wind and his eyes were bright.

"Will you marry me, my love? Will you be my wife?"

The words held the song of his soul in them. "Yes, oh yes. Wasn't I always yours, Owen?"

For the first time I saw myself on my island, happy in my own little world, lost there, in ignorance of the big world that stretched beyond. And way out in a faraway village in a strange, distant country a little boy learned and grew and lived only for me. And the winds of time tore our worlds from us, and set us adrift in search . . . in search of each other . . . questioning, yearning, hungering . . . finally whole, drawn together by forces of love that were stronger than life, as mysterious and sweet as eternity.

His fingers ran over my face. "You're so lovely, Anna. So lovely, so dear to me."

I rested safe in his arms, safe on the cold, wind-swept mountain. Together we talked boldly of a life of our own and called down our dreams.

Chapter Twenty-Three

We set a date for late in March. The sooner the better. The holidays were upon us now and the cold weather was not our friend; it conspired against us. Waiting was timeless torment. We made our minds up that when the weather broke, that would be the signal to us. As soon as it was safe to drive the mountain passes to the Endowment House in Salt Lake, we would go.

Like a ghost, like an echo of last year there came a letter, gray and stained and far-traveled. A letter from home. It arrived the day before Christmas. My father read it, read the frail, shaking words of his father with shaking voice.

I have been ill much, but I am well as I write this letter. The same things happen here season by season—

He told us the news of friends and neighbors we had known.

Anna, your little friend Halldor is now a mother. She was married a year ago to Sveinn Olafsson—you should remember. The best fisherman on the island. You ought to know she has named her new daughter Anna in honor of you and in spite of her father's wishes.

I looked away, unable to hide the emotion his words called forth.

I grow old. There is no way of telling if tide and time will bring you news of your father again. So I say with my heart, God bless you, my children. Hold fast to the things you know to be right and true. Hold fast to what is Icelandic within you. May nothing rob you of that, I pray—

If there were more words written neither Petur nor I heard them. He held my eyes in a look of malicious triumph. I met his gaze, not caring how much the pain showed in my own. He even said something to me later; he could not resist it.

"In your stubbornness you defy everything, everyone, Anna. Even Grandfather—"

I had been thinking about this. My heart had an answer for him.

"Yes, even Grandfather said, 'Hold fast to the things you know to be right and true.' That's what I'm doing, Petur."

He started to bluster.

"And I'm more Icelandic than you are. Tell me, when is the last time you read a book in our language? I read Icelandic, I write Icelandic, I sing in the choir. I tell the old stories to Sina and Haldora at night. I do the fine handwork my grandmother taught her daughter." I turned from him with contempt. "You disgust me, Petur. You have grown into a prudish old woman. I feel sorry for you."

I left quickly before he could answer. I knew my heart now. I had gazed deep into myself with an uncompromising eye. I knew the course I had set was not light or easy. I knew I must meet all doubts and all fears; I must want to do this with every fiber of my being. And so it was. I had gazed at Owen with wide-open eyes and had not found him wanting. I could trust him. Every time I needed him he had been there. I knew he would always be there for me, for the rest of my life. I could respect Owen; I was safe with Owen. And then there was the poetry and the song . . .

Christmas came and went. It was difficult for me. There was a sense of strain in our family and it brought me pain. No lips but Petur's accused me, and yet I knew. In my prayers I pleaded for a Christlike patience and a heart that was quick to forgive, and the power to love.

I did love. I saw nothing but beauty around me, for I carried always in my heart the love of a man—the tender, worshipful love of a man for a woman. It ennobled me somehow. Even Petur backed away and disapproved from a distance. I lived my days in the gentle, protective halo of Owen's love.

Spring came: the rains and the floods, the washed-out bridges, the concern over plowing and planting. I bided my time. The sense of peace and protection still sustained me.

But as the March days came full and round I knew sudden misgivings. Petur's wedding was planned for May. I was sneaking before him—stealing his thunder, jumping the gun, as they say. And all the giddy talk and excitement for Petur and Gudrun. I was to have none of that. No congratulations, no joy, no giggly questions, no fuss over me. I worked quietly on the dress I would wear at my wedding. I worked only in bits and snatches and hid the dread secret in the folds of a thick northern sweater beneath my bed.

When I was with Owen it was all right. Nothing else would matter. The trials came when I was alone in the dark still nights, or perhaps at meeting when I looked around at the kind, open faces that could not know the happiness they were denying me.

I knew what Owen wanted, the dream he held onto. Someday he would be a teacher, a teacher of music. He would fashion instruments with his own hands and teach others to play them.

"There is an old man in Salt Lake," he confided, "who builds violins. He has told me that when I am ready he will teach me."

"Can you play the violin?" I asked.

"I played one as a child. And there are music masters in the city as well. I have talked with some of them."

"Why not now?" I felt my heart soar.

"The time is not right yet. I owe something to my father. He is building his dream, and he cannot do it without my help."

I knew what he was saying. "But the land never releases a man," I protested. "He will eat your dream up with his."

"No, I have my plans set. The time will ripen, Anna."

How patient he was! He could shame me with his patience.

The spring thaw came early that year. A hot sun dried the fields and the mountain torrents. As the time grew near Owen said to me one day, "You should tell your father."

I looked at him with horror. "I can't. He would forbid me and I would be forced to defy him. I couldn't bear to do that."

"I don't think he would forbid you. He may not agree, but I think he would respect your decision."

"You're not taking into account my mother or Petur. Mother is harder to bend than my father, and harder to move. And Petur —Petur would go to all ends to prevent me."

We both knew the truth of that, so we abandoned the subject. Neither of us liked what we were doing, this sneaking off, this deceit, this sense of betrayal. We had both spoken to Owen's bishop, divulging our plans in confidence in order to obtain the recommend we would need to enter the Endowment House. He pronounced no judgment; I think he sensed our struggles. It seemed no other choice was before us. But would we be strong enough to go through with it when the time came?

March was mild. The warm ground responded well to the first spring plantings. There were bees in the air and blue skies overhead. It was time to take Owen's wagon and drive to Salt Lake.

We met the night before on the still slope of mountain. We talked quietly. There was peace between us. We knelt together to ask for the Lord's benediction. His might be the only one we would have, and the one we most needed.

I went to bed at the usual hour and lay there unsleeping. Five more hours and I would rise up from my girlhood bed never to sleep there again. I looked around me at the shadowed familiar shapes I loved so well. This was the home of my childhood, but it was not my home. It had nurtured me and taught me, but now it was time to take up the thread of my own life. This place had colored and woven the pattern of much that was me, but its task was completed. There would be no growth, no new colors and patterns until I broke free and began the next stage of my own creation, the next unraveling of my own life.

I must have slept some, drifting off into dream-stirred slumber. I awoke in the darkness, aware of the chill in the air and the gentle breathing of those around me. I rose with care, moving slowly in the stillness. I felt like a shadow, doing shadowy, unreal things.

The glow from the candle couldn't have startled me more if it had been a whole roomful of lights, or the voice of a skyful of thunder. I turned with a gasp. My mother stood softly haloed, her hair in a braid down her back, her dark eyes misted. She walked toward me; I had no power to stop her. She touched my cheek with a finger that was soft and much warmer than mine.

"A girl cannot wear for her wedding only a plain cotton dress, Anna." She smiled through the tears in her eyes. "No matter how fine and tiny the stitches."

"Mother, how did you know?"

Samuel moved out from the corner's shadow. "I told them, Anna. Please don't be angry. I couldn't bear it."

"Where is Petur?" I whispered the words.

"Petur won't disturb you. I sent him off to help Brother Palsson last night. He spent the night there." It was my father who spoke. My head whirled in confusion.

"You knew . . ." I turned to Samuel. "Did you hear us? Did you spy on us up on the mountain?"

He hung his head.

"How could you? I trusted you, Samuel!"

"You did not trust amiss. Samuel worried about you. When he came to us he said, 'Anna has a good heart. I think you should trust her to follow it, Father.' "

"There isn't much time." My mother was digging around in the big black trunk. "Here, take these, Anna."

In Iceland the women are usually married in black. It was the opposite here, I knew that. The dress I had fashioned was plain white linen with lace at the cuffs and the throat, fine crocheted lace of my own making. I would wear my grandmother's brooch. That was all I had intended.

My mother now held in her arms the fine white veil she had worn at her own wedding, and the silver coronet that fit over it.

"These you must wear. This must be a proper wedding, Anna." She reached in again and drew out the heavy cloak of rich blue cloth with the hand-sewn border of leaves worked in gold and crimson.

"Every woman in my family for the past four generations has been married in this robe. Would you have cheated me of that, Anna?"

I could not speak. What could I say in the face of her love, and my own sense of shame?

We folded the things very carefully for the journey. If we arrived in Salt Lake in good time we would be married early the following morning. Owen had friends in the city we could stay with. It had all been arranged.

We heard his wagon on the road, though he stopped at a distance, silenced the horses, and walked the rest of the way. Samuel had been watching for him, so we were ready.

Father opened the door to him. That was a moment! His eyes grew as round as saucers as he took in the scene.

"I am ashamed, sir, that we did not tell you."

I was grateful to Owen for not admitting then and there his urgings to me.

"I believe I understand, son." My father was trying. I could feel the strain of his effort. "I cannot say I *encourage* this step you're taking—"

My mother came closer and rested her hand lightly on my shoulder. "You're an Icelander, Anna, in every true sense of the word." I looked into her eyes. "For us the harsh, the unknown, the struggle—"

I found myself in her arms and the comfort there was something new and satisfying.

We walked to the wagon, our footsteps the only sound in the gray morning air. I held tightly to Owen's warm hand. My heart was singing. I could go now without that tugging, that torture inside. I could give myself to him freely. I had no dark worries, no doubts, no sense of fear—only gladness inside.

Chapter Twenty-Four

The marriage was all that it should have been, all I had hoped for. I felt regal walking to the Endowment House with Owen, the silver coronet on my head, the rich cloth about me. For the ceremony I wore only my simple dress and my mother's veil; the pure simplicity was fitting. There was a stillness, a sense of reverence as we knelt and took vows more sacred than anything I had known existed. My parents had been sealed here in the Salt Lake Valley soon after our arrival. My thoughts were drawn back to that time and my feelings then as we had knelt in our turn beside them, and were sealed as a family that time, death, or separation could no longer destroy. How little I had understood! Now I knelt as my mother had knelt, as a woman, across from the man I loved, with his hand in mine, and all our tomorrows before us.

Those first few days together we walked the streets of Salt Lake choosing where we would most like to live and imagining what it would be like. We were carefree as children. Owen introduced me to Brother Stephenson and his violin shop, and I understood what drew his spirit there. We drove out by the lake, and the sight of water, the sound of the small waves slapping the white sand brought tears to my eyes. It seemed to restore some ancient rhythm inside my being. We sat for hours beside the lake and sang songs together—some we had taught each other in Welsh and Icelandic—songs that spoke all our hearts felt and could not speak.

The smallest thing we did together was cause for pleasure, even choosing what food we would eat for dinner that night, or packing our things to load onto the wagon, or simply standing together and watching the moon chase the night shadows back into their corners.

At last we drove home. Only then, on the quiet drive south, did Owen tell me what had happened with his own family.

"I told my father. I woke him the morning we left."

I knew by the crease of his brow that he feared my reaction.

"What if he had stopped you?" I breathed.

"He couldn't have done that." There was a smile in Owen's voice. "And I think he knew it. I had written a note to leave—but

I couldn't do that. It worked better this way, Anna. He gave me his hand and thanked me for giving him some time to get used to the idea and . . . to prepare my mother against our return."

Those words cast the first shadow across our days. *Owen's mother.* She had hated me before. What would happen now?

"She doesn't hate you," Owen urged with his usual insight. "She is hurt and afraid just like you, Anna. If you remember that you'll be all right."

I had no idea where we would be living until Owen pulled up there. He had told me all along that he wanted to keep it as a surprise. He tied a scarf around my eyes for the last few miles. When he stopped the wagon and pulled the blindfold off I saw the old Stoddard cabin—but I would not have known it as such.

It was bright and new. There was a window caulked in the old hole, a new door on the hinges, and the whole thing had been whitewashed over. No sagebrush remained. The whole front of the house had been cleared and flowers planted, and a gingham curtain hung from the window, a soft sea blue.

"That's what I've been sketching," Owen explained, "the plans for this place—and carvings for here and there."

I kissed him. "It's been ours in some ways for a long time. Trust you, Owen! But how did you do it?"

He only grinned. "I got it for a good price," he boasted.

He carried me over the threshold and kissed me soundly. "Now, if this were Wales," he said, "there would be a grand party, with cakes and drink until dawn and a piper playing." He set me down with a little sigh. "But at least we are home."

We are home. I echoed the words in my mind. "That's all I need, Owen. Look what you've done!" I clapped my hands and looked around me with joy. My own dishes were in the cupboard, a shelf held my treasures, I recognized the coverlet on the bed. There was even a neat stack of wood piled ready to make a fire.

"I conspired with Samuel the morning we left," Owen admitted. "Otherwise we would have all this to do ourselves—" He stretched out his arm and his face showed his pleasure. But my eyes were drawn elsewhere.

In a corner all by itself sat the Celtic harp. There was something about it . . . even sitting perfectly still it did not seem silent. It brought a spirit of its own to the little room, a spirit too old to name and too sweet to resist. When I looked on the harp I saw Owen—I felt Owen.

"Even when you are out working," I said, as I touched the smooth carvings, "if I am here alone with this harp, you will be here, too."

"There's something you've missed." He pulled me away very gently. He opened a cupboard. Sitting all by itself was a round wooden bowl. Its smooth, shiny skin was covered with beautiful carvings—Viking signs and symbols of ancient design. I lifted it down and held it to me.

"My father," I whispered. I leaned against Owen. I felt my joy was complete. "I could never be happier than I am at this moment," I confessed.

"There will be happier moments even than this. I promise you, Anna." He kissed my hair where it touched my forehead. "But hold on to this. It will help you through times less happy and more humdrum."

I smiled. I tucked the moment far back in my heart like a treasure, and turned to light the fire and cook our first meal in our own home together.

March was a windy month, but Owen assured me that a windy March was a sign of good crops. His father had leased him some land that he worked for our profit, and he still helped his father with his and received a percentage. He worked long, hard days, but our evenings together unwound the hard days into sweetness and pleasure.

We talked and we read, and I sewed while he played the harp, and we sang together. And we adjusted to each other with ease. There were little things, surely, but they fell into place. Owen knew me so well, and could sense my every need. When my long days were boring and I grew to feel awkward popping in on my mother day after day, it was Owen who spoke to Miss Fletcher and arranged for me to help with the older students in the afternoons. Miss Fletcher was pleased with the arrangement and so was I. I even received some small payments in kind, and it pleased me to think that I had earned it myself, to think I was helping, and at the same time doing something I loved.

My father and mother were relieved, I think, as each day went by. Owen's father came sometimes and would chat on the doorstep. His dark, stern looks masked a pleasant interior; he was gentle in his ways like Owen and soft of speech. He even found little things to praise, and I loved him for that. Neither of his older sons had made homes in our valley. Perhaps he valued Owen's help and loyalty. I might not be just what he had wanted for this youngest son, but he did not reject me.

Samuel came nearly every day. Samuel was my sunshine, my substitute for the friend and confidant all girls need. At times he brought Gesli and Sina with him, and that was nearly as good as home. Sometimes even Mother would walk over with little Haldora and visit for a spell, or allow me to tend the child while she ran some errand. Bit by bit the small warmths crept in.

But not so with Petur. Petur held tight to his wrath. He would not give way. He had let my mother know that when he was married—in proper Icelandic style and good Mormon grace—I was not to be invited. I tried to let it pass over me, this anger and this unkindness. And I knew I had given him new fuel to fan the flames: Sunday meetings I attended in Owen's ward.

This was a difficult thing for my father, but at least he would talk with me about it. And strangely enough, it was my mother who spoke out with her stubborn common sense.

"She's a wife now, Einar. A woman goes with her husband's people. That is the way. Besides," she added, and her eyes held a sparkle of challenge, "isn't it one and the same? Aren't all of us Latter-day Saints?"

My father knew how hard it was for me. He took me aside, up behind the house on my mountain. "Are you doing all right, Anna?"

I thought of Owen's mother who marched silently past us without a word, and then silently out again when the meeting was over. I thought of the stares and the whispers, the ones who took their lead from her.

"It's not bad, Father. Some of them aren't unkind. If I didn't have Owen—" I smiled in spite of myself and my father noticed, and I don't believe it displeased him, this show of my love.

"I miss the Icelandic as much as anything, Father. But then I sing the old songs with Owen at night and I still read my books—"

"You do? You, you sing . . . with Owen?"

"He's a very fast learner. And he's good with languages, Father. Oh, I can memorize the Welsh, you know that. But he picks up the Icelandic words and their meanings and can put them together much better than I."

My father's mind was going around in circles, trying to get a picture of this to hold on to.

So we got past the Sabbath, which was just as well. There wasn't much good we could do in discussing it, anyway. It takes people time to accept changes, even the small ones. I would gaze up at the massive, age-old hills and try to remember that. But it hurt nevertheless.

I had taken to wearing gingham dresses and aprons more like the others. I suppose I really wanted to fit in. I saw no reason to retard the process of acceptance when perhaps I could help it. Owen had bought a lovely dress and bonnet for me in Salt Lake. So at meetings I held my own with the most fashionable of the Saints.

But none of that made too much difference as long as Marged kept her stony silence against us. For a while Owen just ignored her and went his way, but that only made it worse.

He came in from the fields one night looking dark and stormy. He was seldom like that.

"What is it?" I asked.

He washed his hands with quick, jerky motions. He could hardly tell me. Agitation seemed to prickle along his skin.

"My mother is ill."

"And just why should that make you angry?" I tried to speak lightly. He glanced at me gratefully, mindful of it.

"It's her way, Anna. She can't get to me any other. She wants me home."

Something cold went through my insides, like a drink of ice water. "Wants you home. What does that mean, exactly?"

"Unreasonable things. She's been plaguing my father for me— small things I can do—used to do for her that no one else does for her now. Picky, pathetic little things—" He held his hands out in a hopeless gesture it hurt to see. "I didn't know this, didn't know she was so extreme—"

He sat down at the table and I began to serve up the food. That jogged his mind. "She cooks my favorite foods, and then acts confused and wounded when I am not there to eat them and praise her efforts." He shuddered. "My poor father, he even suggested that I go there once a week just to humor her."

"Well, you could go visit her," I said. My voice sounded breathless.

"I could and I will," he said, "when this struggle is over. It is a tug-of-war we're in and I can't let her win. I don't dare . . ." His voice held such pain in it.

"What can we do?"

"Anna, Anna . . . I've told my father that we'll come—both of us—once a week."

I was so relieved that the prospect seemed almost pleasant. He could see that in my eyes.

"Don't be fooled, my Anna. She will be cruel. She will try us both."

"She will most likely ignore me. That's what she does at meetings."

"And it's far from pleasant. In the intimacy of her house with her eyes upon you and the power all in her hands—it will be torment, Anna."

Owen was right, as I found out only two days later. We went to Owen's house as he had agreed. Brother Davies opened the door for us and sat us at table and tried to make small talk between us. Without him—without him I shudder to think.

Marged Davies fussed around her boy almost like a young woman whose beau has come to dinner. She anticipated his needs, she plied him with questions, she hung on his every word. And she ignored me as though I were not there at all. It was almost eerie. I watched her as if from a distance, outside the scene. And an amazing thing happened. The hate I felt for her melted of its own accord. I watched its going with a sense of wonderment. What was happening here? A sudden sympathy, a tenderness rose up inside me for this poor, unhappy woman who needed her son and feared the girl she believed would take him away.

Without this strange new sympathy for the woman I couldn't have endured it. She went on and on and it seemed we would never escape.

"Brother Evans brought me a large sack of barley carried over by a recent group of Welsh immigrants. He saved it for me just as he promised."

"I do love barley," Owen admitted. "Do you like it, Anna?" His continuing efforts to draw me in. It seemed almost tasteless to me, but I knew Owen loved it. I had cooked it for him myself.

"You and Bronwyn. I've never known any who craved barley like you two. Barley cakes for breakfast, for tea, barley soup for supper. That was the one thing Bronwyn would cry for on the ship. How she did miss her precious barley."

And that was the other: everything that wasn't Owen was Bronwyn. She spoke of the girl as though she were still living, surely still a strong presence influencing every act, thought, taste, and desire of Marged's day.

"I must get out that picture and rehang it, Owen. Remember, the one that fell and broke last May? It was Bronwyn's absolute favorite—I didn't mean to neglect it!"

By the end of the evening my mind was exhausted as well as my nerves. We walked home together not speaking, grateful for the silence. I didn't know how much Owen was suffering until he said, "How can I ask you to forgive me, Anna? I'll never submit you to that again—I didn't . . . realize . . . what I was asking." His voice nearly faltered.

"It's all right," I said, fumbling to reach for his hand in the darkness. "Really, it is, Owen. I don't know why, but something happened—something inside myself—" How could I say it?

"She's not an easy one to put up with, much less understand."

"She's your mother, and she loves you so desperately, Owen. And she's afraid, just like you told me—"

He stopped on the path, right where we stood, and kissed me. "I love you, Anna. More than I did last week—" He laughed. "More than yesterday . . . more than ten minutes ago."

His lips found mine again, and I forgot all about where we were or that someone might see us. I was lost in the touch and intensity of his love.

Chapter Twenty-Five

It was April but it felt like late May; it felt warm as summer. We were still going to Owen's house at least once a week. I was growing used to Marged's ways; they did not offend me anymore, or even get on my nerves very often. But this past week everything she said or did seemed to hurt my feelings. I found myself fighting back tears and I didn't know why.

I still taught every afternoon; it was one of my pleasures. And it helped to know that Miss Fletcher's need for me was sincere. We had gone through a bad day or two and I felt exhausted. It was time to walk home, but instead I sank into a chair.

"I can't face the idea of walking that distance," I told her.

"You haven't been feeling well lately, have you?" She acted concerned.

"I guess not. Sometimes I get dizzy—light-headed. And the smallest things make me tired, and my stomach's upset, especially in the mornings—"

Miss Fletcher laughed, a lilting, happy sort of laugh. "Don't you know what's wrong, Anna?"

I looked wide-eyed; I felt ridiculous.

"Couldn't it be . . . could you possibly be . . . do you think you are pregnant, Anna?"

It flooded over me then. Of course! I should have suspected. I had wondered a little, but couldn't believe. My face went as red as a beet.

"Don't worry, Anna. You're very young to know for certain about such things."

She was kind and eased me away with skill from the embarrassment I was feeling. I walked home in a state of awe. Should I tell Owen? *How* should I tell him? I decided to wait. Another week or two. But a few more days convinced me that Miss Fletcher's intuitive reasoning had been right. I had better tell Owen before he figured it out for himself.

Still I hesitated. There never seemed a right moment. It was such a momentous thing to simply blurt out while we sat eating dinner. And afterward, singing or cuddling close to the fire, I somehow couldn't make the words come out, couldn't break the spell.

There came a night when I decided I must get it done, one way or another. After the dishes were washed up and put away the faint light from the window seemed to draw me. "Let's go for a walk," I suggested, and Owen was quick to agree.

There was such fragrance in the air I could almost taste it. I closed my eyes and let it wash over me, sink through my skin until I felt as if the light throbbed inside me and shone through my eyes.

"There's something happening with you, Anna. What is it?" Owen spoke the words very gently. Still, I looked away from his eyes. I wanted to say, "Guess! Go ahead, please, and guess it, so I don't have to say the words out loud."

But I couldn't do that, and I couldn't avoid his gaze. I looked at him as evenly as I could. "I believe . . . well, as far as I know . . . I . . . we're going to have a baby, Owen."

He just stared at me. "This early? Have you talked with your mother?"

I had thought of that. "I wanted to tell you first."

Only the hint of a smile touched his lips. "This is sooner than I had expected."

What was the matter? Didn't he want this child? I fought the tears I could feel in my throat and behind my eyes. I had thought he would be overjoyed.

"I'm sorry, Anna. I didn't mean for this to happen so early to you—"

What did he mean?

"Heaven knows, you have enough on your hands already." He looked beseechingly into my eyes. "Do you mind too much? Will you be all right, Anna?"

"What do you mean, Owen? Am I all right? Do I mind?"

"You seemed . . . distressed. I thought . . ." He stammered a little. "Perhaps you might not want the baby!"

"I not want a baby! Of course I do. Any time, under any conditions. I thought it was you! You acted unhappy when I told you—" I felt the tightness inside loosen its grip and gently release. "Oh, Owen, I was so worried that you were unhappy."

"Never!" He grabbed both my hands and swung me around. "A child of your and my making. A miracle, Anna."

It was all happiness then. It was magic between us. We skipped and laughed our way home. The fair night had grown chilly. Owen settled me comfortably and wrapped a blanket about my legs and sat at the harp and played music to me and the baby.

"He can hear us," he said with confidence. "I know he can."

I believed him because I wanted to. Somewhere inside me a new, distinct human person was being formed, with ears and nose all his own, with his own way of speaking. Would his mouth smile the way Owen's did? Would he have my eyes? Would he laugh at life or be timid, a thinker, a dreamer?

We dreamed our way through the night together, aware of the child in the same way that one is aware of the perfume of flowers within a room, or the wind in one's hair, or the faint sound of birdsong in the morning when the mind is still clouded and the notes hold a muted, liquid quality more felt than heard . . . like vague echoes of music known in some long-ago time, never quite forgotten.

Petur's wedding was a splendid affair, or so others told me. I was ill that morning and stayed in bed. I felt sorry for myself and cried a little. I had asked Mother not to tell Petur about my child. I felt he might somehow spoil it with his contempt. I wanted no angry accusations to rest upon it: this small, perfect, unknown creature I carried inside. I wasn't sure even how my parents felt at the prospect. It certainly couldn't be construed as unconditional joy. They were kind, they tried to show interest, enthusiasm, not the concern that kept rising behind their eyes.

We decided not to tell Owen's parents. Owen worked the long, hot summer days and I languished. There was little else I could do. I did not feel well. There was no teaching to challenge me out of my lazy complaisance. I kept the house up, I cooked Owen's meals, I tended the garden. I was too proud to let those things go.

But I dreaded Sundays. I longed for someone there to confide my secret to. Someone whose eyes would light up when I told them. Someone else who would care. Very soon it would show. And then I would have to tell Marged and then, somehow, the magic that Owen and I had kept contained within our four walls would seep out, would die, would disintegrate in the harsh light of Marged's knowing.

As it was, Owen told them for me. He knew how I felt, how afraid I was. It seemed my fears were well founded. He told his mother and father together. She just blinked her eyes. She would not face the subject directly. When Owen pressed her she started talking about her own pregnancies, her own children's births. It was eerie. I felt the strangeness of it pass through me. It chilled me in spite of the heat of the August night.

Petur and Gudrun lived in the dugout on the bench together. I didn't like to think of her living there. Perhaps unconsciously I went to visit my mother less often. I hated running into young Gudrun there. It was awkward when we two met; I didn't like it. There was too much between us to even make small talk. And, of course, the one thing I most dreaded loomed over me: What if I were to meet Petur there? I couldn't bear the thought of what might happen. I couldn't face a confrontation with Petur now. Thus as a slow yet natural process my visits lessened, and my sense of isolation and loneliness increased.

Perhaps in some ways Owen was right—it had been too early. I was still struggling to make a place for myself, indeed, to decide who and what I was. Was it too early to worry about the happiness and identity of a child?

"What will this baby be?" I asked Owen one evening.

He looked up at me perplexed. "Either a boy or a girl. At first I thought a son would be fine, but I'd like a daughter. A little girl who looks like you."

"That's not what I meant."

His brow wrinkled in worried lines. "Well, what is it, then?"

"If I bear you a son, will he be a Welshman? Will he think and talk like a Welshman? Or somewhere inside will he carry the legends of Iceland?"

"How can I know? How can anyone know, Anna? We'll have to watch him. He will very likely have some of both."

"But if I have a daughter I will *want* her to be Icelandic like me. I will want her to talk and dress and think Icelandic."

"That's all right. You'll meet no objections from me."

"You're not the only one concerned. What of your father— not to mention your mother." He was beginning to roll his eyes at me. "And Owen, what if she's not Icelandic? What if her makeup is totally Welsh?"

"Anna, Anna, all these what-ifs are driving you crazy. There's nothing we can do about anything now. This child will be his own person, whatever that is. And you and I will love and help him the best we can. We can't do more than that—not now, not ever."

He was right; I knew he was right. But my feelings had never been subject to reason. The reason was fine. But it was his tenderness and love that would see me through.

Autumn came, and with it the restlessness autumn brings me. I missed singing in the choir. I hadn't been back, not once since my marriage, though Owen had urged me to return. I was afraid. At the base of my fears was Petur. I could just see him striding in there like judgment itself, with his long finger searching me out: What, a traitor here? You must not admit her. She is no longer fit or worthy to stand in our midst.

"Sing in the other choir with me, then," Owen persisted. I couldn't think about that without trembling inside with fear. Now the coming child was a natural excuse. But that didn't help me, because what I wanted was to sing, and to be with people, people I liked and felt at ease with. Sometimes I despaired. Would I ever again belong, and feel that belonging?

Thank heaven I did have something that I could do. School was in session again, and I taught my classes, despite my increasing size, despite aches and pains, and a sense of shyness that at times overtook me as I bent over a student's desk or stood in front of the classroom, aware suddenly of what my profile must look like to them.

But the teaching wasn't enough. I took to writing, page after page of poetry, too much in English. Why the flow came in English instead of Icelandic I didn't know. Sometimes I even attempted to redirect it; then it would stop altogether. I took long morning walks, once the sun had cleared the mountains. The poems would write themselves out in my head, crowding line after line, until I took to carrying pencil and paper with me and huddling cold on the least likely rock just to sort them out.

The ones I considered good I rewrote into my notebook, the one my parents had given me when I turned eighteen. Just over two years ago. I had been a child then, facing a whole new world full of challenge and colored by fear. I was doing the same thing all over again. But some things were different. I was no longer a child, though I felt so at times. I had a husband to help me through, and I had a baby coming who would expect me to be wise and strong and self-denying like my own mother. I couldn't picture myself that way. Could this baby be happy with a mother who was still half child?

The snows came in early November. The air, dry and cold, burned my throat when I breathed it. We were expecting the baby anytime after mid-December. It was hard to tell, hard to pin it down exactly. But that still meant weeks — only weeks left before this new child came into my world.

My mother sewed little things for the baby and assured me that she would come whenever I called and stay as long as I liked. I was glad for the things I had learned in taking care of Haldora. Still, the idea of a child of my own was a frightening thing.

Marged still attempted to ignore the entire issue. For her I did not exist, so how could the child? If I spoke to her directly, if I asked her a question, she ignored me as though she were deaf, as though I had not spoken, as though she could see right through me. I stayed away. I even stopped going to meetings. The weather was wicked. I was nearing the end of my time. Owen didn't push.

"When this child is born can we move to Salt Lake?" I would ask him.

"Moving to Salt Lake has nothing to do with the birth of this child."

"It has to do with a miracle that just isn't going to happen."

He would gaze at me with deep, steady eyes that I couldn't read. "Then I will stay here. I'll buy land from my father and work it and build my instruments here."

My impatience would show in my face, but I couldn't budge him. "I will not leave here without what you call the miracle, Anna, not ever."

Only then, only at such times was I angry with him. Only then did I feel there were ways we were separate still.

Christmas in Wales is a much different thing than it is in Iceland. And Owen loved, with a childlike delight, to celebrate. He taught me to make plum pudding and oat cakes and a form of wassail; we dressed a yule log for the fire; he carved small toys and found children to give them to. We bundled up and went caroling with a group of Welsh singers whose voices were as tuneful and clear as bells in the crisp winter air.

"I miss the church bells," Owen would say to me over and over. "In our village every church had a belfry, high and black. When the ropes were pulled all at once and the bells started singing—each with its own solemn note—there was nothing like it. I used to close my eyes and pretend I could ride on the swell of that music straight up to heaven."

We took gifts to Owen's family. His brothers came. They were kind to me and gracious, but not like Owen. Owen's sparkle and charm were his own, and they set him apart. And though Marged seemed happy to see her older children, her attentions were still centered on Owen, and everyone knew it.

It was actually easier for me with a group there. I slipped into the background and Marged's neglect was covered over. His brothers' wives were nice girls; they drew me into their conversations and asked questions about the baby. How good it felt! I found myself wishing that they lived closer.

Near the end of the day Owen took me to see my parents. He had made little toys for Gesli and Sina and Haldora. It was such fun to watch him down on the floor playing with them, making them laugh at his silly antics. It was such a nice feeling to sit in my old home again, eat my mother's cooking, and hear the soft voices I loved raised in the songs of my homeland.

We were ready to leave. Ten more minutes and we would have been gone and it wouldn't have happened. We were standing outside the door when Petur and Gudrun drove up in their buggy. The young ones were making snowballs and pelting Owen, until Samuel laughingly took his side and a regular battle ensued. I could see little Gudrun tugging insistently at Petur's sleeve. But his face was set. The horses hardly slowed as he turned the carriage and drove on past the house. The children waved and shouted, as children will do, unaware and unknowing. I stood in the snow and cried like a child; I couldn't help it. My father held me against his warmth.

"Anna, my Anna, don't let him break your heart this way."

I choked on my tears. "You can say that, but you don't know what it's like." He held me tighter.

"It is his pride that prevents him now. In his heart he knows that he is the one at fault. But he can't admit it. He can't humble himself to ask forgiveness of you."

"Then what good does it do him to go to church every Sunday, pay his tithes, and preach from the pulpit with hate in his heart?"

"It is not hate he feels, but remorse. He is human, Anna. In some ways he tries to do right, in some ways he is good."

I would not concede that. I blew my nose into Mother's hanky.

"If he goes to church, if he does his duty, someday something might touch him, might change him inside and give him strength to conquer this thing that is wrong in his life."

Yes, of course. But until then . . .

I went home with Owen. He was tender, so tender with me. We sat and sang, and when he felt that I had calmed down some he told me, "I have one last present for you, Anna. Would you like it now?"

"Yes," I said. I needed something.

He hesitated. "It's an unusual sort of present. Here—close your eyes." He tucked the quilt around my legs. "Are you comfortable? Keep your eyes closed—just a minute."

I could hear him sit down at the harp. The faint whisper, the promise of music stirred through the strings as he touched them. He played a few chords. They were light and exquisite. He added the words:

> Sometimes when daylight sifts to gray,
> And all the world lies silent

His voice was as soft as a child's, with that purity in it.

> We listen to the stillness sounds
> That seem to seep from underground
> And weave a warmth around us . . .

His voice wove a spell for the words, of his melody's making. He drew me into his spell. I felt light as a feather.

> Sometimes when winter crackles cold,
> We snuggle near the fire

My eyes flew open. I swirled in the spell. These were *my* words! Where had he found them? What had he done? He continued singing, his own eyes closed, one with the music.

> And mother reads of olden days,
> Her voice like silk; a golden haze
> Transports me back to other days

His voice made each word a pearl. There were tears in my eyes.

> And I know feelings soft and new
> That taste like dreams and promises come true.

He prolonged the melody with the harp strings. When the music ended it vibrated through us still. Owen opened his eyes. He could see from my face how thoroughly he had transformed me, how magnificent was the music of his creating.

"You wrote the words in your book," he said. "You once read them to me. Otherwise, I would not have intruded." He came and knelt down beside me. "They cried out for music, Anna. I had to do it."

I couldn't speak. I pulled him close. "You've given my own words to me," I whispered. "You've made them live! You've shaped my spirit into melody—"

"No, the music was there. I released it, that's all. I just gave it voice."

That's all!

I don't know how long we sat there together. It began to snow outside and the room grew still. But loath to destroy the spell we sat wrapped in each other, warmed by the silent music inside our hearts.

Chapter Twenty-Six

I had wanted the child to be born on Christmas. When the first day of the new year came I thought, *Now, surely now!* I went to bed that night discouraged. When the gray darkness woke me I lay in its comforting folds and knew: *It has come.* I woke Owen. He saddled the horse and rode for my mother. Mother first, the midwife second.

They told me it was easy, for a first birth; perhaps that was so. Mother and the midwife stayed right beside me, but in the next room Owen sat at the harp and played. That is all I remember. He played the Icelandic songs I had taught him; he played his Welsh love songs; he played the tune he had set my words to, the voice of his heart. My daughter came into the world to the sounds of her father's music.

He scarcely gave them time to clean and wrap her, then he whisked her away and laid her in the cradle beside him and continued to play. And I drifted off with his music. In the peace of that music I dreamed, and the dream was real. And the dream changed my life forever.

When I awoke I remembered each scene, every smallest detail. And I knew that the dream had changed me. I felt it inside. I felt it must show on my face and be heard in my voice.

When they left us alone for a while Owen brought me my baby, laid her into the nest of my arms.

"She was born on the second day of the new year." He beamed. "That's a good omen, Anna."

"Tell me about it," I smiled.

"You're just humoring me."

"No, no, I want to hear it."

"Well, in our country a child born on the second day of January is destined to be handsome, wise, and happy."

"Do the fairy folk will it so?"

"Tradition has it that it is so from time before knowing."

I touched the petal-soft cheek. "So it will be with her."

"Have you chosen a good, long Icelandic name?" He winked mischievously at me. "I could stand to call her Anna, myself."

"In Wales," I began, "the mother is said to have the privilege of naming the firstborn."

"That's right. How did you know?"

I knew more than that.

"Name her what you will," he repeated.

"Thank you," I said.

The time had come for him to go tell his parents. I knew he was fearful. I kissed him gently and sent him away with a prayer in my heart.

He was gone for a very long time. When he walked through the doorway his face was washed of all color. His eyes were dull. The baby was fast asleep. I pulled Owen to me. "Tell me, tell me what happened."

It took him a while. But at last he could make the words come.

"I told them," he said, "just simply: Anna had the baby. A beautiful girl. She is healthy and well. I hadn't expected much—"

"I know—"

"But when *nothing* happened, something in me seemed to snap. I took my mother and shook her hard. I said, 'Mother, I can't bear this! You are driving me mad. The girl I love, the girl I married has just had a baby. It is *my* baby.' She did nothing. Her eyes grew wide and she clasped her hands."

" 'Do you hear me, Mother?' I cried. 'My wife and my child. You must admit that they exist, you must accept them.' She did not speak. I just said without thinking what came to my mind."

"What was that?" I urged.

"I stood back and told her that if she did not want Anna and my child, she could not have me. I had borne her cruelty to you longer than I should have. I would not watch her treat my child the same way—I *could* not watch it! It was breaking my heart to watch her—"

"What happened then?"

"She began to cry." He held his hands out in that helpless gesture I had seen before. "She cried and cried; it was awful to watch her, Anna. Such anguish in her weeping. When she was through she dried her eyes and looked up at me—with such simple meekness."

"Did she say anything?"

"No. I kissed her and left."

"It will be all right," I told him. He didn't think so. But I knew something he didn't know, and I hoped and believed . . .

We set the date for the baby's blessing. We invited our families and special friends, some from Owen's ward and some from the Icelandic group on the bench. I didn't worry about it. The dream had brought me a peace that allayed my fears.

But in spite of the dream I was not the first to make a change. It was Gudrun who showed up on my doorstep one morning. I let her in. I took her to see the baby, letting her hold the tiny, pink-clad body. She crooned and petted, then looked at me with child-like eyes.

"Are you pregnant?" I asked.

"Yes," she replied. "That's why I came, Anna. I've been cheated long enough."

That set me aback. "Cheated? What do you mean?"

"The other Icelanders—all of them—love you, Anna. You have so many friends. They miss you, they talk about you, they sing your praises. I am lonely. I have wanted your friendship—"

She paused for a breath. I straightened the blankets around the baby. My fingers trembled. I had been so consumed with *my* loneliness and *my* pain.

"So I have come . . . if you will have me . . ."

What could I say? I drew her into my arms and we wept together, but the shame still stayed in my heart. Tears can't wash shame away. Only deeds will push it out of the heart, replace it. Heaven granting, I would have many chances to work out the shame.

"I will be there," she said as she left. "I've already told Petur that I will come when the baby is blessed—with or without him."

"You are brave," I said. "If he lets you come, that is something. Don't expect . . . don't expect a miracle."

But I knew that I was expecting a miracle of my own; I was praying for it.

The day dawned mild and sunny. I bathed my child and dressed her in a long, soft gown of my own making and hummed her father's music into her ears.

Our two-room cabin was small. We had decided to bless the

baby at Owen's house, and his father agreed. We could all fit there, Welsh and Icelanders alike.

Even then it was crowded. But it was a nice kind of crowding. We sang a hymn, "The Spirit of God," all four verses. When it had ended there was no one in the room except Latter-day Saints, all one mind and one spirit.

Gudrun sat beside my mother; Petur was not with her. He had been torn when she left without him, she had seen that much. Her pleadings seemed to have touched his heart, and that gave her hope. At least she was here, and her eyes were happy. My father and Owen's would stand with him in the circle when he blessed our child, as well as Brother Palsson and Brother Sveinsson and Bishop Evans and Brother Morgan and one or two others. His mother sat near the front of the room with her husband. I sat beside Owen. When the song had ended I stood on my feet.

Only Owen knew what would happen. He smiled at me gently, encouragement in his eyes.

"In Wales," I began, "the privilege is given the mother to choose the name for her firstborn child. If a male it is after her family. But if a girl-child she takes the name from the father's family."

The room went still. My listeners seemed to lean forward with interest now.

"This custom is strangely in keeping with a dream I have had." I looked at my mother. She smiled at me with her eyes. "When my child was born, right after the birth," I continued, "I fell asleep to Owen's playing, and I dreamed a dream. In my dream I saw a ship that was crossing the ocean. On the deck of the ship a small group of people huddled around a coffin draped with a Welsh flag. The people were crying bitterly. One young woman threw herself over the coffin and would not let go—"

Marged gasped and her hand went to her throat. Owen moved beside her and held her other hand in his.

"As I looked I could see the face of the dead girl. She stood by the coffin—she hovered in the air just beside the woman and gazed on her with love—"

"No, no, you couldn't have seen that!" Marged cried. She turned in her chair to face the others. "The girl is lying. Owen told her the story; he told her what happened, that's all."

I moved forward a step or two so I stood before her. "It is a true dream, Marged," I told her. "I saw it well. I am not a dreamer of dreams, but I saw her so clearly. Her hair was like burnished copper as it fell down her back and lay in long curls on her shoulders. Her brow was fine, her skin very white and fair, her nose long and slender, her eyes large with thick black lashes. As she smiled upon you, I saw that one eye was brown and one eye was blue."

Marged sat very still. She looked at me sharply. "You saw that difference? It was hard to discern; very few people did. Owen didn't know that about Bronwyn." She gazed at me a long moment. "What else did you see?"

"I saw a fine locket around her neck of an ancient pattern—a cross, I believe, with some kind of wreath woven around it. She lay cold in death with the locket against her throat." I swallowed.

"Go on," Marged said. Her voice sounded normal.

"You combed her hair out with long, gentle strokes, and you placed her hands. Then carefully you removed the locket from about her neck and tucked it inside your own bosom."

Marged's eyes grew wide. She rose from her chair and walked out of the room. All our eyes followed her movements and held. After a long moment she returned. She held something clasped in her hand. She walked over before me and opened it wide for our eyes to see.

Lying against her outstretched palm was a dainty locket wound with a fine golden chain. It was the same locket I had seen in my dream—the locket Bronwyn had worn when she died.

"They meant to bury her with it, but I couldn't bear that. It was all I had of her to keep! No one knew I took it. I never told; I never showed anyone." She looked at her husband. "Not even Mervyn, through all these years."

She stretched out her hand. "For you, for the child," she said.

I took the necklace from her. Her fingers closed warm over mine. "For Bronwyn," I said through my tears. "The child's name is Bronwyn. It was always meant to be so."

I sat down by her side as Owen rose and took his daughter from my mother's arms and walked forward. One by one the brethren joined him and formed a circle, their hands in unison bearing up the child in the sacred order of the priesthood.

The door pushed open. Petur stood there. I didn't see him until Owen's father leaned over and nudged me. I think I cried out. His eyes were for me and me only.

"Am I too late?" he asked.

He read my answer in my eyes. He stepped into the circle. Owen held Bronwyn cradled in his hands. With the power of the priesthood he gave her a name and a father's blessing, as was his right. There was poetry in the words he used when he blessed her, and the Spirit's benediction on all he said.

I opened my eyes. Owen brought my daughter to me and placed her into my arms, which ached at the touch of her.

"Marged," I said, "would you like to hold your granddaughter?"

"Oh, yes, if I might." There were tears in her eyes and mine. I leaned forward and kissed her. She pressed my hand until it hurt. I pulled gently away. I knew Petur was standing alone, waiting for me. I went to him, into his arms.

"Please forgive me, Anna."

I can't bear to watch a man cry. "Don't cry," I pleaded. "You are my Petur again. You've come back. That's all that matters."

There was happiness then, in such measure I scarcely could hold it. And music inside my head and in Owen's eyes.

There was a surfeit of joy. I was glad when it ended, when I found myself alone with Owen and Bronwyn. I liked the name. It was an ancient name. It felt warm on the tongue.

"She looks like you," Owen said.

"No, she doesn't. Just look at those eyes. They're round like yours, and I swear there's a sparkle in them."

We gazed down on her. "Did you know," I said, "that for one thousand years the land of Iceland has been lived in and loved by my people."

He was impressed. But my thoughts were pushing elsewhere. I remembered the man who had paused in his busy, important life to welcome a strange, shy Icelandic girl to Zion. A man who had stood before his people with tears in his eyes and said: *There is not another nation under heaven but this, in whose midst the Book of Mormon could have been brought forth. It was the Lord who directed the discovery of this land—and the victory of the colonies, and the unprecedented prosperity of the American nation up to the calling of Joseph the Prophet.* Why did I feel, as Brigham Young felt, that this land was mine?

"Bronwyn may have a Welsh name," I said, "but she isn't Welsh."

"Oh, I'm certain of it," he agreed, his whole face a wide grin. "Her mother's far too Icelandic for that."

I laughed at his teasing, but tears threatened again. "No, no, she isn't Icelandic. She's *American*, Owen. America is such a new country, and look at Zion—it is an infant, just like her. They'll grow up together."

He saw what I was saying.

"They're both brand new, unspoiled—" I struggled for some way to say it. "Like a clean white page not yet written on."

"With endless possibilities." Owen liked that.

She was my daughter. She would carry Iceland within her forever, and the poetry of Wales would dance in her eyes. But she was Zion-born, a covenant child, and she would walk in a world very different from mine—a world I was helping to create, a world I was part of—a world in which I wanted to belong.

"A Utah-born Latter-day Saint," Owen murmured. "One of the first of her kind."

There was poetry in it, and the strain of countless worlds that had gone before, the pride and power of generations stretching back beyond time.

I was at peace with that thought.

"Will you play for me, Owen?"

I sat at his feet with my child in my arms. The harp music murmured, then sprang into melody. But even its wild, happy singing could not match the joy of the song in my heart.